CW00351115

IMAGES OF
SHREWSBURY

FROM THE COLLECTIONS OF SHREWSBURY MUSEUMS SERVICE

DAVID TRUMPER

SUTTON PUBLISHING

Sutton Publishing Limited
Phoenix Mill · Thrupp · Stroud
Gloucestershire · GL5 2BU

First published 2006

**Shrewsbury &
Atcham**
Borough Council

British Library Cataloguing in Publication Data
A catalogue record for this book is available from the
British Library.

ISBN 0-7509-4261-4

Typeset in 10.5/13.5pt Photina.
Typesetting and origination by
Sutton Publishing Limited.
Printed and bound in England by
J.H. Haynes & Co. Ltd, Sparkford.

*This book is dedicated with love to my grandson,
Samuel Radford*

Title page photograph: The town from Millington's Hospital, *c.* 1890. This superb photograph was taken from the top of the hospital tower looking towards town. From the top, left to right are the spire of St Mary's, the water tower, St Alkmund's, St Julian's and the Victorian market hall. One arch of the Welsh Bridge can be seen in the centre. The white buildings to the right of the bridge are the Circus Inn and brewery. The site was redeveloped by Morris's between 1919 and 1924 with the circus building becoming the firm's main warehouse. The cottage behind the pony and trap at the bottom of the drive is the Cooper's Arms. Behind the wall is St George's School, which was founded in a small room in Chapel Street in 1834 by Dr Robert Darwin. A larger school was built behind the infants' and was opened by headmaster John Bill on 28 June 1880. The children of Frankwell proved very difficult for the new master, who wrote a month later, 'The work sadly too much for the teaching power. So over powered I could scarcely keep on.' However, the school prospered under Mr Bill and new classrooms were added before the boys moved out to a new school across the drive in 1897.

CONTENTS

Abbey Foregate, 1918. This view of the abbey church and the Foregate was taken by an air crew training at the Observer School of Reconnaissance and Aerial Photography at Monkmoor Aerodrome. The house in the bottom left-hand corner was once the home of the Carlines, a family of stonemasons, whose handiwork included the English and Welsh Bridges, Lord Hill's Column and St Michael's Church. The house was transformed into Shrewsbury Technical College in 1899 and was replaced by a modern building in the 1930s, which is now the Wakeman School. Across the road is the Congregational church that was designed by George Bidlake of Wolverhampton and opened in 1863. In 1972, with the amalgamation of the Congregational and Presbyterian churches, it became the United Reformed church. The bridge to the rear is the railway viaduct that was built for the opening of a route down to Ludlow in 1852 and on to Hereford the following year. Until 1835 the main road out of town was to the left and at the rear of the abbey, but in that year Thomas Telford drove his new London to Holyhead road through land to the south of the church, destroying what remained of the chapter house, dormitory and cloisters.

INTRODUCTION

During the second half of the nineteenth century three notable societies were founded to explore and document the history, archaeology, flora and fauna of Shropshire and the surrounding countryside. They were the Shropshire Archaeological Society, which was established in 1877, and the Caradoc Field Club and the Severn Valley Field Club that amalgamated in 1893 into the Caradoc and Severn Valley Field Club.

To entertain and inform members and to educate the wider public, lectures were given during the winter evenings that were illustrated by lantern slides. These views were deposited with the Shrewsbury Museum and now form the bulk of that collection.

Herbert Edward Forrest who was born in Wolverhampton on 18 May 1858 and educated at Shrewsbury School was one of the pioneers of lantern-slide lectures. The early part of his working life was spent in banking before he joined his brother in the family music business. In 1883 they bought the business of J. Boucher at 37 Castle Street and traded under the name of Forrest and Son until 1919 when his brother retired and he became sole owner. His love of natural history led him to join the Birmingham Natural History Society, becoming joint Honorary Secretary in 1878. Two years later he was elected a Fellow of the Royal Microscopical Society.

After his move to Shrewsbury Forrest joined the Caradoc and Severn Valley Field Club, where he became 'the life and soul' of that organisation. He was the Honorary Secretary of the club until 1929 when he became President, a post he held until his death in 1942. His first book, *The Fauna of Shropshire*, was published in 1899, the same year in which he helped to reorganise the town's Natural History Museum and became its Honorary Curator of Zoology. Eight years later his second book, *The Vertebrate Fauna of North Wales*, was published. In recognition of his valuable contribution to natural history he was elected a Fellow of the Linnaean Society in 1930. He joined the Shropshire Archaeological Society in 1914 and spent an amazing amount of time researching the histories of some of the county's ancient houses. This research led to the publication of *The Old Houses of Shrewsbury* in 1911, *The Old Houses of Wenlock and the Wenlock Edge* in 1915, *The Old Churches of Shrewsbury* in 1922 and, outside the county, *The Old Houses of Stratford-upon-Avon* in 1925. In 1923 *Shropshire in English History* was published for use in schools. The book was developed from a series of lectures he had given in 1922 ranging from the Roman period to the coach and railway days of the nineteenth century, which he hoped would be told as a story, taking youngsters away from the dry history of monarchs and dates and getting a new generation interested in local history. In 1924 *The Shrewsbury Burgess Roll* was published, and owing to this and the help that he had given the Borough Council concerning the history of Shrewsbury over many years, Forrest was made an Honorary Freeman of his adopted town in 1938.

An aerial view of Shrewsbury taken from the south, over Belle Vue and Coleham, at a height of over 10,000ft, *c.* 1938. Apart from a narrow strip of land in the top right-hand corner the Severn acts as a moat and almost completely encircles the town. Between the two arms of the river the castle was built to protect the only land route into Shrewsbury. The trees in the centre, along the river, shade Victoria Avenue as it sweeps around towards St Julian's Friars. Above is a large section of the town wall that enclosed the town in the thirteenth century. The Bridge on the right is the English Bridge, and just above is the new Technical College and the Gay Meadow where Shrewsbury Town Football Club play their home games. Note the open ground (bottom left) at the junction of Belle Vue Gardens, Kingsland Road and Longdon Road, which has now been built over.

A contemporary of H.E. Forrest was John Arthur Morris, a local man whose father Thomas Morris had founded a building firm in St Austin's Friars. He was educated at Newport Grammar School and followed his father into the family business. His interest in construction led him to research and document old buildings and to carefully restore them. He was also interested in the humbler dwellings of our ancestors and was a great advocate for retaining old cottages and bringing them up to modern requirements. His great knowledge of the county's buildings made him a popular speaker and an adviser to the Borough and County Councils. He joined the Shropshire

Archaeological Society in 1899, was elected a member of council in 1914 and later Vice-President. He also contributed many interesting papers to the society's transactions and collected the memories of many of the town's older citizens. He was involved with the careful excavations at Wroxeter and the repairs to Sutton church and was a member of the Roman Roads Committee and Honorary Curator of the Archaeological Department of Shrewsbury Museum. In recognition of his services to Shrewsbury he was also made an Honorary Freeman of the Borough. Shortly before his death in May 1940 he was elected a Fellow of the Society of Antiquities.

Following in the footsteps of Forrest and Morris was Llewellyn Cyril Lloyd, another adopted son of Shrewsbury. He was born in Nottingham in 1903 and came to Shrewsbury in 1931 to assist his father in running the *Shrewsbury Circular*, which he took over after his father's death in 1943. He joined the Shropshire Archaeological Society in 1933 and served on its council for many years before becoming a vice-president. He was also a member of the Caradoc and Severn Valley Field Club, acting as Honorary Secretary from 1940 until 1956 and as President from 1954 to 1955. He was a founder member of the Shropshire Conservation Trust, a member of the Ornithological Society and a Fellow of the Linnaean Society. From 1946 he was a tutor for adult classes organised by the University of Birmingham he trained the official tour guides of Shrewsbury and was a co-opted member of the Victoria History Advisory Committee. He also acted as Honorary Archivist and Curator to the Borough of Much Wenlock, and shortly before he died he and his students produced a number of excellent articles to commemorate the 500th anniversary of the Borough's first charter. He also produced a number of papers that were published in the *Archaeological Transactions*, wrote *Shropshire Fauna* with co-author E.M. Rutter and produced *The Inns of Shrewsbury*, which is still essential reading for all local history enthusiasts. Lloyd died suddenly at his home in Cardeston on 23 August 1968 at the early age of sixty-three.

Unlike Forrest and Morris, Lloyd was a talented amateur photographer who would have used his own lantern slides to illustrate his lectures whereas the other two would have relied on professional photographers and colleagues to produce the illustrations for their talks. Forrest undoubtedly would have used J. Laing, a photographic artist whose studio was next door to his own establishment. The business was later taken over by R.L. Bartlett, who provided photographs for the local printing firm of Wildings which produced the town guides for Shrewsbury and published all of Forrest's books.

Many fine views of the town were taken by W.W. Naunton, co-owner of the printing firm Adnitt and Naunton, the premises of which were in the Square. Both men were members of the Archaeological Society, Mr Adnitt occupying the post of Honorary Secretary and Mr Naunton the post of Auditor. Another professional photographer was James Mallinson whose studio was in Frankwell. He recorded in great detail two major developments in the town for the Borough Council. The first of these was the alterations to the English Bridge between 1925 and 1927 and the second was the demolition of buildings in the Barker Street area in the 1930s for the creation of an inner ring road and car parks. Many of the photographs were put on to lantern slides that were deposited at the museum.

An aerial view of Shrewsbury from the south-west of the town, *c.* 1938. Bottom right is the rear of the Crescent on Town Walls. Moving left is the Methodist chapel, the High School, the concourse to the Kingsland Bridge and the Eye, Ear, and Throat Hospital. Centre left is the Market Hall, which was opened in 1869, and above the Cattle Market that was opened nineteen years earlier. The large building in the centre is the Music Hall with three of the town's churches above; St Julian's on the right, St Alkmund's in the centre and St Mary's to the left. Just below St Mary's is the old round water tower. To the right of the river as it snakes its way out of town at the top are the two rows of poplar trees that once lined the Castle Walk. Most were killed when the land on either side of the walk was raised and soil and debris was piled around their trunks.

Two excellent amateur photographers whose slides have been preserved at the museum are Herbert John Gornall, an electrical engineer who lived in Abbey Foregate, and the Revd Charles Drinkwater, vicar of St George's Church in Shrewsbury for fifty-one years. He was well known for giving illustrated lectures in St George's School in an attempt to educate the poorer people of his parish.

For many years this vast collection of photographs, which also includes views of Shropshire, Wales and other historic sites around Britain, have been stored at the museum and used occasionally for research purposes. Today, after being cleaned up and digitally enhanced, 3,000 photographs can be viewed on Shrewsbury Museums' 'Darwin Country' website at www.darwincountry.org.

1

Around Rowley's House & Mansion

Bridge Street from Barker Street to the Welsh Bridge, *c.* 1930. The buildings on the right were demolished in the 1930s for the inner ring road and a car parking scheme, but the houses on the left survived a little longer. The man on the right is standing outside Richard Taylor's grocery shop. Mr Taylor was known as 'Sticky' as he sold small bundles of sticks as kindling for 1*d.* Between the man and the ladies is the Old Ship Inn, first recorded in 1780. In 1900 the inn was owned by Trouncer's Brewery, but the landlord was able to brew his own beer so long as he purchased thirty barrels a year from the brewery. It was called the Old Ship to distinguish it from the New Ship Inn in Hill's Lane. At their annual general meeting in 1936 the Shropshire Archaeological Society passed a resolution asking the council to preserve the inn. Unfortunately the resolution was ignored and the building was demolished in 1937.

Bridge Street, c. 1930. These cottages stood opposite the Old Ship Inn on what was later the multi-storey car park site. Bridge Street was once part of a larger area known as Romaldesham which was named after a small chapel dedicated to St Romald. There are references to the district as early as the twelfth century. This site was once occupied by a substantial timber-framed house called Romaldesham Hall and was lived in for several generations by the Montgomery family. They were tanners by trade and a number served the town as burgesses. At the front of the house was a large porch that protruded 6ft into the street. The giants Gog and Magog were depicted on the floor of the hall where there was also a large chimney breast inset with stones depicting the arms of the town and family. When the mansion was demolished in about 1760 the stones were reused over the doorways in the new buildings, and when they were knocked down in 1949 they were left to the museum in Rowley's House.

Hill's Lane, *c.* 1945. The camera is pointing towards Mardol. The building at the Mardol end with the two eaves is still there, but the buildings down to the corner were removed in the 1960s. They were occupied by the Gullet Inn, which was first recorded in 1780 as the Seven Stars and then as the Little Gullet. It was there that the Gullet Club was founded in 1785. Members met every Tuesday evening between 6 p.m. and 10 p.m. and contributed *2d* each that was put towards a quarterly dinner. In 1835 an electoral address was given in the form of a poem by Benjamin Poole from the Gullet parlour. The last verse ended:

> To have each member and the chair protected,
> The half-pint rounds and finds so justly claimed,
> He knows that all these qualities shall please,
> And cause each gent to smile rather than frown,
> Elect him MP,
> And then, he at ease,
> Will order the half-pints to guzzle down.

The inn closed in 1942 and was used for a number of years as a canteen for Midland Red bus drivers and conductors.

Left: Claremont Street, *c.* 1865. This busy scene was captured just before the demolition of the buildings on the corner of Claremont Street and Mardol. The tall timber-framed building was one of several fine houses that were demolished on the market site. It was four storeys high and had an elegant gable at the Mardol end. The last occupant of the building was Henry Thomas, a grocer, who was born in Alberbury. He was in business there until October 1866 when his stock, which included spices, sugar, tea and coffee, was sold off. The shop across the road in Mardol, which is now Brigg's shoe shop, was occupied by Charles Thomas, a draper.

Shoplatch, *c.* 1866. This photograph was taken across the new market hall site to Shoplatch. The buildings on the left lead towards Mardol Head, while the building on the right is on the corner of Market Street. Shoplatch is a derivation from the place or residence of the Schutte family who lived close by. Below the tall building in the centre is the entrance to Drayton's Passage, which takes pedestrians through to Market Street. The smaller building to the left of the passage was a coffee house and dining rooms occupied by Thomas Jones. In 1896 a large five-storey hotel and dining rooms was built on the site. The building on the corner of Market Street was occupied by George Goucher, a boot and shoemaker.

Opposite, bottom: Barker Street/Hill's Lane, *c.* 1935. In 1930 plans were drawn up for an inner ring road and central car park in the Barker Street, Bridge Street, Belstone and Hill's Lane area, to help alleviate the growing traffic problem in the town at this time. The area was full of congested housing that could only be approached through a series of passages, and in most cases the conditions were very insanitary with people living in appalling circumstances. These properties were approached from the passageways leading to the New Ship Inn from Barker Street or Hill's Lane. The roof on the extreme left in front of the timber-framed house overlooks Barker Street. The buildings stood on the site of the Midland Red bus station and were demolished without being properly surveyed and recorded. The timber-framed building was a substantial property that was built up against the New Ship Inn. The building in the centre, although greatly dilapidated, is very interesting and is causing a great deal of speculation among local historians. Its English bond brickwork and traces of Tudor mullion windows have led people to surmise that this house could pre-date Rowley's Mansion as the first brick-built building in Shrewsbury.

The Market Hall site, *c.* 1866. From the middle of the nineteenth century it was decided that Shrewsbury needed a market hall large enough to accommodate all the smaller markets that were scattered around the town. However, it could not be agreed where the new hall should be sited. The debate went on for years and was often referred to as the 'Battle of the Sites', until the area bounded by Shoplatch, Belstone, Claremont Street and Mardol was finally chosen. After the demolition of the buildings on the site all that was saleable, such as doors, window frames, oak floorboards and bricks, was stacked in lots and sold at auction. The buildings behind the workman are in Mardol. The timber-framed building was occupied by William Franklin, who was listed as a bird and animal preserver, or taxidermist. The buildings on the right are in Mardol Head. Note the rounded building on the corner of High Street and a fine-looking timber-framed house in the distance at the bottom of Pride Hill.

The Market Hall site, *c.* 1866. Two gentlemen with their backs to Mardol pose for the photographer during the demolition of the old buildings on the Market Hall site. Work on clearing the site was said to have proceeded briskly and the whole area was cleared by the end of 1866. The last census taken in the area in 1861 tells us that over 300 people were living there in 59 houses. As well as living accommodation the site contained 29 shops, 16 brewhouses, and 2 public houses, the Kings Arms in Claremont Street and the Mermaid in Shoplatch. The businesses also covered a wide variety of needs and included a tailor, watchmaker, hairdresser and dentist. The bricks and timber are being stacked in the foreground in readiness for the auction in May 1866, when Thomas Edwards, an auctioneer and valuer with offices in Mardol Head, was offering over 100,000 bricks and large quantities of building material for sale. The buildings on the left are in Claremont Street, but none survive today. Note the message on the staircase, 'Please do not sit here'.

The new Market Hall, *c.* 1868. The new hall begins to take shape, showing the distinctive blue, red and white brickwork enhanced by the Grinshall stone dressing that made the building so attractive. The rounded tops to all the windows and doorways were also a pleasing feature. The building was designed in the Italianate style by Robert Griffith, the county surveyor for Staffordshire, and was erected by Mr Barlow of Stoke-on-Trent. A number of stone urns and finials decorated the building as well as some fine carvings. They included the arms of the town over the Mardol entrance and a copy of a cornucopia depicting Peace and Plenty by the sculptor Landucci over the entrance to the corn market on the Shoplatch side of the building. The foundation stone of the new market was laid by the Mayor, J.T. Nightingale, on 24 January 1867 and was opened twenty months later by Mayor Thomas Groves on 29 September 1869.

Rowley's House, *c.* 1932. This is the side of the house facing down towards the Welsh Bridge, with Hill's Lane to the left and Barker Street to the right. Note that a brick building has been built right up against the house, wattle panels are exposed and large holes have been blocked by tin sheeting. Arthur Ward the Borough Surveyor recorded that 'there was little or no glass, and few frames in the window openings. The staircase, which was dated 1641, was removed to America some years ago. The timbers in the walls of the ground floor, most of which had decayed or been removed, had been replaced by rough brickwork. The ends of some of the projecting floor beams on the first floor had rotted or cracked and these brick walls supported them.' The small lean-to on the left is a wash-house, which would have been shared by several families living in the area.

Above and opposite: Rowley's House, *c.* 1938. From the outset it was agreed that Rowley's Mansion should be saved. Many people knew about the mansion, which was erected in 1618 and is reputed to be one of the first brick-built houses in Shrewsbury, but few people knew of the greater gem that stood at the rear. Rowley's House was so obscured by surrounding buildings, which in some cases supported the old house, that it was hardly visible. The house, which was occupied by Morris's and used as an oil store, was described by H.E. Forrest as 'terribly dilapidated; almost ruinous'. But as the buildings around it were removed it was obvious that this house was also worth saving. After adapting the plans for this area of the car park, the structure of the house was slightly altered by putting a passageway through the centre of the building to give access to both car parks and by setting back part of the ground floor to allow a pavement to be put in on the Barker Street side. The upper storey there was held up using six beams salvaged from other houses in the area. The house was also completely renovated using material gathered from the surrounding buildings and was converted by the Borough into a museum.

Hill's Lane. *c.* 1920. The Street was named after John Hill, a descendant of the Rowley family and Mayor of Shrewsbury in 1689. The iron fence at the top of the street was in front of the Methodist chapel, which was opened by John Wesley on 27 March 1781. The next pair of houses were in front of the New Ship Inn that was approached through the passageway in the centre. The house to the right of the passage was once a lodging house occupied by Francis Jones. Next door is Rowley's Mansion. In the eighteenth century it was occupied by Dr William Adams, the vicar of St Chad's. He was a fine scholar and counted among his friends Dr Samuel Johnson, who visited him there in September 1774. By the nineteenth century the area had become very run down and the mansion was converted for commercial use. In 1808 it was being used as a woollen factory and in 1886 auctioneer Herbert Rogers advertised 'The Old Mansion Auction Mart, Hill's Lane, Shrewsbury. Always open for the reception of Household Furniture and other Goods. Sales By Auction Every Monday.' At the beginning of the twentieth century it was used as a warehouse by Richard Downes, a wholesale hardware merchant. In 1983 the mansion was restored by the council and converted into part of the Borough museum.

2

Shrewsbury Townscape

The Railway Forecourt, *c.* 1905. This view was taken soon after the completion of
the new forecourt. The original height can be seen where the people are standing
behind the gas lamp. They are on a path leading up to a flight of steps on to the Dana.
Before the alterations the shops behind the wall opened directly on to the forecourt.
The largest building was occupied by Thomas Wardle, a fish and game dealer, whose shop
closed during the alterations. The smaller building housed William Tudman's tobacconist
shop while the one on the extreme right was occupied by the brewers Allsopp and Sons.
Both continued to trade there. Looking down over the station and guarding the only land
route into the town is Shrewsbury Castle. The windows and the chimneys are the work
of Thomas Telford who transformed the castle into a dwelling. The building was
occupied at this time by the Downwood sisters.

Castle Gates, *c.* 1900 The street takes its name from the two town gates that stood at either end of the road. The outer gate was situated just below Meadow Place and was known as the Castle or North Gate. The upper gate crossed the road just below the steps to the Dana and library on the right. This gateway was the largest and was known by several names, the most common being the Jersey Gate. During its history fourteen inns have occupied buildings on this short street. This rare view of the Nag's Head, which stood on the corner of Meadow Place, was in existence from 1780 to 1927. In 1900 the inn was owned by Dorset Owen who lived in Oswestry. Over the door was a fine, carved wooden sign, which was the work of John Nelson, the sculptor responsible for the two lions at the Lion Hotel.

Opposite, bottom: The gatehouse to the Council House, Castle Street, *c.* 1920. This is a view of the rear of the gatehouse looking back towards Castle Street. It is a fine Jacobean house that was built in 1610 by Sir William Owen of Condover. It has all the embellishments of the best timber-framed houses being built in Shrewsbury at that time. One of the finials at the front of the building depicts a knight in armour. The figure once held a key, symbolic that the house was once used as a lock-up for prisoners brought to appear before the Council of the Marches when it was being held at the Council House. The building through the arch in Castle Street is the Grosvenor Hotel, which for many years was known as Thomas's Temperance Hotel.

Right: Castle Street, *c.* 1930. Two ladies and a boy stop to admire the triumphal arch that has been erected at the entrance to Shrewsbury Castle for an unknown event. The timber-framed house behind once stood on the site of the Guildhall on Dogpole and was the town house of the Newport family. It was moved to this site at the end of the seventeenth century soon after Lord Newport had been created Earl of Bradford. To the right is the Presbyterian church, which was built in 1870. It was named St Nicholas's Church after a medieval chapel that had occupied that site in the outer bailey of the castle. It was designed by Robert Bennett of Weymouth in the Romanesque style.

Castle Street, *c.* 1890. This view looks up Castle Street towards Pride Hill. The timber-framed building on the corner of School Lane is Palin's/Plimmer's cake shop and restaurant. Just above is the sign of the Ark for John Franklin's fancy repository, and further on the long frontage of the Raven Hotel. The building on the right still stands but the ground floor has altered quite dramatically over the years. The boy is standing by Mrs Sarah Dutton's house, a large property with two sets of windows on either side of the door and three storeys high. She was the lessee of the refreshment room on Shrewsbury Station. The house next door was occupied by Thomas Jones, an auctioneer and farmer. WHSmith opened a store there in 1906 and completely changed the ground floor when the store was expanded in 1938. The large building on the left is Thorne's Mansion. Although the frontage was fairly modern there was evidence of a much older building dating back to the beginning of the seventeenth century. The Thornes were an old Shropshire family had served the town as bailiffs and as members of parliament. In 1756 the mansion was leased to Sir Edward Smythe of Acton Burnell and his niece, the celebrated Mrs Fitzherbert, the morganatic wife of George IV, who is reputed to have been born there. The building was demolished in 1921 to make way for Shrewsbury Co-operative Society's new registered office and central store.

Opposite, top: Castle Street. *c.* 1900. A horse-drawn carriage known as a growler picks up a passenger outside the Raven Hotel one day at the beginning of the twentieth century. Across the road the second building from the left is the fishmonger's shop of F. & T. Hammonds. Note the royal warrant over the door, which was acquired for providing Queen Victoria with fresh fish, game and poultry while she was staying near Bala. The shop to the right was occupied by Richard Mansell who also had premises on Wyle Cop. William Lowe was listed as a decorator, but before he moved there the shop was occupied by Frank Newton, who later moved across the road. The two properties to the right of Mr Lowe were occupied by the Alltree Brothers, who were advertised as general furnishers, builders and estate ironmongers. The next building is the Vaults, an alehouse that was occupied at this time by Henry Guntrip. The inn was first recorded as the Bull in 1804 and later Morley's Wine and Spirits Vaults. It was delicensed in February 1927.

Right: Pride Hill to Castle Street, July 1903. The mock high cross was erected on the site where the body of the rebel Henry Percy, known as Hotspur was exhibited after the battle of Shrewsbury in July 1403. The four-storey building in Castle Street was a ladies' clothes shop called Bon Marche. The business belonged to Arthur Dyer who was listed as a linen draper, silk mercer and milliner. He acquired the shop from Ledger & Ledger and continued in business there until about 1929 when it was converted into a Marks & Spencer's. Two doors further down is the large top hat hanging outside Frank Newton's gentlemen's outfitter's. The firm was known locally as the Big Hat and originally traded on the opposite side of the street.

Pride Hill, July 1903. Flags are flying in Pride Hill to mark the week-long programme of events that ran from Sunday 19 July until Saturday 25 July. The varied programme included church services, Shakespearian plays, a public luncheon in the Music Hall, historical lectures and excursions and a fête in the Quarry that included old English sports. The highlights of the week were the anniversary service held on 21 July in Battlefield church and Shakespeare's *King Henry IV, Part One* that included scenes of the battle. The first building on the left is the Clarendon Hotel that occupied the site of an old timber-framed inn called the Market Tavern. By 1929 the Clarendon had closed and the ground floor had been converted into a clothes shop with the upper rooms becoming an extension of the telephone exchange out of the post office next door.

The Crown Hotel, St Mary's Street, *c.* 1940. The first Crown Hotel was recorded in a Georgian building on this site in 1780. This mock-Tudor building was built by the Church Stretton Hotel Company and opened in August 1901. In July 1907 a new billiard room was opened at the hotel by the Mayor, Thomas Corbett. This photograph was taken during the Second World War; note the sign pointing the way to the air-raid shelter and the first-aid post. In 1940 the hotel was closed and the building was used by the army as headquarters for the Mid-Western Division and as a residential club for British officers. The hotel did not revert to civilian use until March 1948. The Crown was demolished in 1962 to make way for a concrete and glass office block and shops known as Crown House.

Opposite, bottom: St Mary's Street, July 1903. This photograph can be accurately dated as the wooden cross was erected at the busy junction of Castle Street, Pride Hill and St Mary's Street during the celebrations for the 500th anniversary of the Battle of Shrewsbury. Note the garlands hanging across the mock-Tudor frontage of the Crown Hotel that had been opened just two years before. In the official programme for the celebrations it is advertised as 'a First Class Family and Commercial Hotel, opposite the Post Office and three minutes from the Railway Station'. It also promised a 'Revised and Exceedingly Moderate Tariff'. To the left is Vincent Crump's confectionery shop. Like Plimmer he was able to supply the famous Shrewsbury Cake, which according to historian Henry Pidgeon had been presented to distinguished visitors since the reign of Elizabeth I. In 1832, when the Duchess of Kent and Princess Victoria visited Shrewsbury, they were 'graciously pleased' to accept a box from the Mayor. The building on the corner of Castle Street was occupied by John Jones, a draper, but within a few years would be converted into the United Counties Bank Ltd.

Warwick House, Dogpole, *c.* 1945. Beneath the plaster there is a fine early seventeenth-century timber-framed building. Until the 1940s it was a private house lived in by two sisters, the Misses Lloyd. It was then transformed into the Warwick, a private residential hotel initially run by H. Bradbury. The hotel then passed to F. and E. Trow who advertised 'a licensed restaurant with a full menu and fresh salads'. The accommodation offered at this time was fairly basic, just bed and breakfast, with hot and cold running water and an electric fire in each room. In 1961 the hotel was sold for £6,000 to a London development company, which wanted to demolish the old building and erect offices and a showroom on the site. A Ministry of Housing and Local Government Inquiry was held at Shrewsbury Castle on 7 November 1961. The argument for demolition was that the building was unsafe, that the front was 'an abortion' and that the area where the house stood was 'not attractive and on either side of the building there are places of no outstanding character. It is a bastard street.' A.T. Morris, the Borough Surveyor, said, 'To demolish Shrewsbury's old Warwick Hotel would be little short of vandalism.' Thankfully, the inquiry agreed with him and within two months the property was sold to Jack Williams who turned the hotel into a health food shop and café called Healthiways. Today the building is a popular restaurant and small hotel called Cromwells.

The Lion Hotel, Wyle Cop, *c.* 1920. Built on one of the busiest roads leading into the town, there are records of the Lion dating back to the beginning of the fifteenth century. The left-hand section with the open gallery is the oldest part of the hotel and dates to that time. The top section was altered after the arrival of Robert Lawrence and most of the work, including the beautiful Adam-style ballroom and assembly room, is attributed to local architect Thomas Farnolls Pritchard. As well as developing the hotel into a fashionable social centre, Lawrence also established the Lion as one of the principal coaching hotels in the country and was instrumental in changing people's minds on the route of the London to Holyhead road, bringing it through Shrewsbury instead of Chester. At the beginning of the twentieth century there were two shops situated in the lower section: the left-hand one was occupied by Breeze Ltd, a coal merchant, while the shop next door housed a bazaar belonging to E.A.G. Foulkes.

Wyle Cop, *c.* 1890. This is a wonderful view of the sweeping curve between Mytton's Mansion on the left and the brick Inland Revenue Office, which is now part of the Lion Hotel, on the right. The end section of the mansion once housed an ironmonger's shop belonging to Blower and Jenks and then to Shuker & Son. The lean-to on the right has been replaced by a mock-Tudor building, which housed one of Morris's grocery shops. The next-door building housed W. Webb, a cabinet maker, upholsterer and cattle food manufacturer, and also the Compasses Inn. The impressive timber-framed house to the right is called Henry Tudor House, as he is said to have lodged there in 1485. The section to the left of Barrack's Passage is the London & Liverpool Fish Warehouse, which was run by William Roberts. He advertised in 1886 that he had in daily, 'a good supply of all kinds of fish, game and poultry in season', and also supplied 'Wenham Lake ice in large or small quantities'. The business was later taken over by Harry Mudd of Grimsby.

Opposite: Belmont Bank to Old St Chad's Church, *c.* 1930. Belmont Bank was formally known as Back Lane and was once connected to Wyle Cop by four shuts or passages. This fragment of old St Chad's Church is all that is left of the ancient building that was demolished after the tower collapsed in the early hours of 9 July 1788, destroying a great deal of the old church. The surviving building is known as the Lady Chapel and was erected in 1496. It was altered in 1571 by Humphrey Onslow, the uncle of Richard Onslow, who was Speaker in the House of Commons during the reign of Elizabeth I. Richard died in 1571 and was buried between the chancel and the Lady Chapel. The building on the left is timber-framed and dates from the Elizabethan period. In about 1790 a brick skin was built over the front, an extra storey was added in the roof, an extension was built at the rear and the timberwork was hidden under a coat of plaster, completely disguising the old building. Towards the end of the nineteenth century it was the home of Mr Hall, who had an auction house in Sherman's Hall, Milk Street. In 1900 the house was occupied by Mrs Wateridge, the widow of one of Mr Hall's partners. By 1917 it was a girls' school run by Miss Helen McGaffin before it was converted into the Granville Liberal Club.

Milk Street, *c.* 1890. This view of Milk Street was taken from the top of St Julian's Church steps. Milk Street is very short and was once part of St Chad's Lane that ran from High Street past Old St Chad's Church down to the town wall. The building in the centre with the raised entrance is the Shearmen's Hall, which dated from the fourteenth century. It became a theatre before being converted into Shrewsbury's first Methodist chapel by John Appleton in 1761 and on several occasions sermons were preached there by John Wesley, the founder of Methodism, and also by John Fletcher, the vicar of Madeley, who was known as the 'Shropshire Saint'. It was also used as a temporary courtroom, a tea warehouse and an auction room before it was demolished in about 1895. The timber-framed house to the right is Proude's Mansion which dates from 1568. The building to the left on the corner of Wyle Cop is also timber-framed but the spaces between the frame are now filled with red bricks.

The junction of the Square and Princess Street, *c.* 1900. This snowy scene was taken from underneath the old market hall in the Square. The timber-framed house on the corner of Princess Street is Lloyd's Mansion which was built in 1570 by David Lloyd a wealthy draper. It was occupied later by Joseph Della Porta, an Italian immigrant who had opened a shop in Princess Street before extending into the mansion. With the extra space he was able to open departments for ironmongery, boots and shoes, sewing machines, bicycles and furniture. Note the sign on the corner for the Central Cycle and Furniture Store. Just to the left of the pillar is the grand entrance to the Working Men's Hall which was opened in 1863. During the 1950s the hall was used by the Shrewsbury Repertory Company for staging plays. To the right of the pillar is the draper's shop that was occupied by Dyas Brothers.

The Crescent, Town Walls, *c.* 1945. This terrace was built of brick to a neoclassical design by Joseph Bromfield, 1795. From the front it has three storeys and a basement, but at the back the ground drops considerably, making it six storeys. The fanlights to the front doors and the matching blind fanlights to the ground-floor windows are an attractive feature. At the beginning of the twentieth century the house at the far end was the home and business premises of solicitors C.D. and R.A. Craig. It was later used by the Shrewsbury United Service Club Ltd before becoming the labour exchange. In 1984 it was transformed into the home of Ebenezer Scrooge's nephew, when *A Christmas Carol*, starring George C. Scott in the title role, was filmed in the town. The ivy-covered house was where Mrs Julia Wightman, the temperance fighter and wife of a former vicar of St Alkmund's, spent her last years. She is reported to have approached her death with great dignity even writing out the cards that would be sent to her friends after her death. The message read, 'Mrs Wightman entered into her rest this day.'

Swan Hill, *c.* 1940. This street name was first mentioned in St Chad's register in 1697 and recalls the Swan Inn that stood on the corner of Cross Hill from about 1671 until the early nineteenth century. Before that the street was referred to as Murivance. The Admiral Benbow on the left was first recorded in 1835 as the Talbot Tap. In September 1853 it was Lot 7, part of the sale of the Talbot Hotel in Market Street, which was being held at the Lion Hotel. The particulars inform us that 'The little inn and premises (formerly the Tap of the hotel) in the occupation of Mrs Harvey as yearly tenant. The house contains six bedrooms, two parlours, kitchen, large cellar, brew or wash-house and coal (back) yard. Also a yard on the north side with extensive stabling and coach houses and a wide gateway to Swan Hill. It measures about 48 feet in front and 126 feet in depth'. The white building below was occupied by A.T. Marston & Company, sanitary and heating engineers.

Grope Lane, *c.* 1930. Grope Lane could be classed as a shut as it gives pedestrians a quick route from High Street into Fish Street. At the top of the lane is the sign for W.B. Walker's printing works, which occupied a large area of Grope Lane and Fish Street. The firm was taken over from Bunny and Davies and in 1936 was the publisher of *The ABC Railway and Omnibus Guide for Salop and the County.* The building on the right dates from about 1575 and was once a public house known as the Cross Keys, the Globe or Newman's Vaults. At the beginning of the twentieth century Thomas Golling converted the inn to a gentlemen's outfitter's shop. It was known throughout the county and beyond as the 'Tie Shop,' as he kept a stock of over 20,000 ties, the largest collection of any private trader in the country. In April 1939 the business was taken over by Bradley's of Chester, who had other premises on Pride Hill. The building was restored in about 1990 and is now a coffee shop.

St Alkmund's Place, *c.* 1938. This is a view across St Alkmund's churchyard to the Burial Shut, a passage leading through to Butcher Row. The tall building belonging to John Blower and the smaller house to the right were demolished in the 1950s to widen the road between Butcher Row and St Alkmund's Place and to build public toilets. The house to the left is now part of the Bear Steps complex; the steps are just out of sight. John Blower was a house furnisher: his business occupied this building and the one behind facing down Butcher Row. Living in the houses at this time were Herbert Nudds, Francis Hall, Hubert Meredith and Edward Attwood.

Fish Street, *c.* 1930. This section of the Bear Steps complex between the steps and St Alkmund's churchyard is known as the Oriel or the Orrel. It was built in about 1601 and is thought to occupy the site of the collegiate building belonging to the church of St Alkmund. By the end of the 1940s the building had been acquired by the Corporation with the view to restoration, but it was left to decay for another twenty years. By 1968 the whole complex was in danger of demolition, but was saved by the newly formed Civic Society which stepped in and restored it. The work was a great success and the society was awarded a Civic Trust award. The top of the building that faces the churchyard is now a popular café while the bottom part on Fish Street is a shop.

Fish Street, *c.* 1910. A man carrying a basket of bread poses at the bottom of the Bear Steps. The boys are standing on the sharp bend that leads up to Butcher Row and just behind them is the rear of the Abbot's House. The artists look as if they are positioned to paint the old buildings on the corner of Grope Lane. They are sitting under part of the Bear Steps building that was turned into an open gallery when the building was renovated in 1968. I wonder if the ladies realise they are sitting in front of two water closets that were used by several families living in the cottages at the top of the steps. The buildings to the left were occupied by Harper's furniture warehouse before becoming part of Walker's printing works.

The junction of Fish Street and Butcher Row, *c.* 1935. An old man takes in the warm sunshine on this quiet corner of Fish Street. The timber-framed building on the left is the side of the Abbot's House. The white building in Butcher Row is the Central Hotel, a gentlemen's commercial hotel. Until about 1900 the building was a private dwelling, but was converted into a temperance hotel by Mrs Elizabeth Jones. The hotel was purchased by the Smith family in the 1920s and for a while Albert Smith ran a dairy from there. It remained a temperance hotel until the 1950s. It was acquired by the owners of the Prince Rupert and has been absorbed into that hotel, this section being the main entrance.

Butcher Row. *c*. 1900. This atmospheric photograph was taken early one morning with the sun shining towards Fish Street. The sign of the aptly named Rising Sun is on the right; it was one of six public houses that have been recorded on the street. It only had a short life from 1883 until 29 August 1908 when it was delicensed. In 1900 it was owned by Henry Gregory of Weston Mill, Oswestry, but run by Robert Davies. It had three public and three private rooms with accommodation for four people in two rooms. The other hostelries in the row were the Butcher's Arms, the Bull, the Cock, the Lamb and the Tankerville Arms; of these only the Bull remains. The tall timber-framed building above the Rising Sun was removed in the 1930s.

St John's Hill, *c.* 1905. This hill is first mentioned in 1529 and was named after the Hospital of St John in Frankwell which owned land and houses in the area. It has also been called Swine Market Hill as pigs were sold there and on Cross Hill before the cattle market opened on Smithfield Road in 1850. The wagons are weighed down with wool waiting to be unloaded for the annual wool sale. The sale was one of the biggest in the Midlands and was organised by auctioneers Hall, Wateridge & Owen. It took place in June or early July and was held in the Market Hall, the Horse Repository in Raven Meadow and in large tents especially erected for the occasion. A variety of fleeces were sold, including Shropshire, Kerry Hill, lambs and crossbred. The number of fleeces varied from year to year but would average between 40,000 and

St John's Hill, *c.* 1900. Two pupils from Shrewsbury School make their way back from town one summer's day. In the background is the Market Hall with its tower that rose to a height of 151ft. Its clock, made by Joyce of Whitchurch, had four faces that glowed green after dark. The round windows below the tower let light into the Corn Exchange. The large building on the right is the side of the Theatre Royal or the County Theatre. It was erected on the site of Carlton Hall in 1834 and was considered 'an important improvement to the thoroughfare leading to St John's Hill and the Quarry, as well as an ornament to the town'. The cottages on the left were demolished in 1915. One had been an inn called the White Lion where Horace Montford, the sculptor of Charles Darwin's statue, was born. Just below is the Methodist church that was erected on this site in 1805 when the Methodists moved from Hill's Lane. The chapel was rebuilt with this fine frontage in 1879.

3

The River Severn

The town from Coton Hill, *c.* 1920. The spires of St Mary's and St Alkmund's can be seen on the skyline. The building on the left is the waterworks, which supplied the households in Shrewsbury with water for domestic use. The water was taken from the river at Coton Hill and pumped to the water tower between St Mary's Street and Butcher Row. The top of the tower is just visible below the spire on the right. The building in the centre with the chimney is Barker's timber yard. It was later taken over by George Phillips who was known locally as Woppy. He was listed in 1928 as a marine store dealer. The land on the right on the Frankwell side of the river was known in medieval times as Goose Land. In 1452 it belonged to the Cole family.

The Welsh Bridge, c. 1920. The new Welsh Bridge was built several yards further downstream than the old one. The Mardol end of the old bridge, which was also known as St George's Bridge, is occupied by the small building just to the right of the house with four windows. It was designed and built by two Shrewsbury men, John Carline and John Tilley, who had just finished working with Thomas Telford building a bridge over the Severn at Montford Bridge. Telford was not actually involved with this project but advised against building on that site as the current would erode the foundations. His advice was not heeded and the bridge still needs regular monitoring and remedial work by divers. The new bridge built out of Grinshill stone has five semi-circular arches, surmounted by a balustrade. It is 266ft long, 30ft wide and cost £8,000. It was opened in 1795 with the first carriage passing over in September while on its way to Shrewsbury Races. The area to the right of the bridge was cleared in 2005 and the site redeveloped into Shrewsbury's new theatre.

The Welsh Bridge, c. 1930. This is a view of the bridge looking upstream towards the site of Frankwell Quay on the left. Nothing remains of the quayside, which was constructed in 1608, as it was probably erected out of timber. The house on the left is now used as offices by Hall's auctioneering firm, but the building has lost its two bay windows. The building on the other side of the bridge is the Frankwell Forge, which was opened towards the end of the nineteenth century by H. and E. Davies, who were listed as wheelwrights and blacksmiths in 1896. The forge had a long life and only closed in December 2004. The long roof line above the forge belongs to the Welsh Presbyterian chapel that was built in about 1850. It was converted into a garage in the 1920s. Behind the fence of railway sleepers, through the second arch from the left, was an area that was known in Frankwell as the Muck Yard where people from the Little Boro used to deposit their rubbish. Just beyond was Penny Hedge, where the women of Frankwell would do your washing and hang it on the hedge to dry for a penny.

Mardol Quay from the river, *c.* 1930. Mardol Quay was set up by Rowland Jenks in 1607 and a great deal of trade was brought into town by this route. Tolls were charged and for every bargeload of coal or wood, 12*d* was paid. For every ton of other goods 2*d* was paid by burgesses while all foreigners were charged 4*d*. The building on the left with the two windows looking over the river marks the site of the original Welsh Bridge. It was also known as St George's Bridge from the hospital of St George that stood on the Frankwell side of the river. The stones of the old quay can be seen below the flat-roofed building – the rear of Gethin's garage – which occupied the site from 1921 to 1958 when it was demolished for road widening and for the planting of a small park. The new office block behind the garage was built for Morris's between 1919 and 1924. The offices front a complex of warehouses, butchery department and bakery, which cost in the region of £30,000. The large chimney in the centre belongs to Cox's tannery.

Mardol, *c.* 1952. The photographer is standing at the bottom of Mardol with Smithfield Road to the right and the quay leading up to the Welsh Bridge on the left. The narrow street opposite was the original road out of town until 1795 when the new Welsh Bridge was built further downstream. Until then the Old Welsh or St George's Bridge, with its picturesque towers and solid arched gateway, would have been immediately in front of the viewer. The building on the left-hand corner is part of Gethin's Garage. In 1896 it was known as Quay House and was the home of W.E. Morris, a house painter. Note the ragged wall on the corner of Smithfield Road; it is the scar left after the demolition of the Hill's Arms that was recorded on the site from 1795 to 1952. Another inn called the Anchor stood five doors down, between 1835 and 1886. The buildings were demolished in about 1960 for road widening and the creation of a park on the site of Mardol Quay.

The Dry Arch of the Old Welsh Bridge, *c.* 1950. The bridge stood several yards upstream from the new bridge, which was opened in 1795. The town side of the old bridge stood opposite the bottom of Mardol while the Frankwell end was to the left of what is now the Chapel Garage. The old bridge dated from the thirteenth century and was also known as St George's Bridge from the Hospital of St George that stood on the Frankwell side. The old bridge was sold at auction and was taken down soon after the new bridge was opened. The dry arch was part of Lot IV and was described as 'the ground on and under each side of the dry arch as staked out, reserving a free passage over the same, to and from the houses adjoining. The purchaser of this lot is to have a free passage 20 ft over Frankwell Quay, in front of Mr Field's warehouse on the River, and to Frankwell as staked out'. For many years the arch acted as part of a cellar to a house erected over it. The house was demolished in the middle of the twentieth century and the arch is in danger of demolition when the new theatre is erected on the site.

Opposite, bottom: The Porthill Bridge, *c.* 1950. The bridge gives a direct route for pedestrians from the suburbs of Porthill and Copthorne into the centre of town. The bridge was built by the engineering company of David Rowell of Westminster in 1922. It was formally opened on 18 January 1923 by the Mayor, Alderman Thomas Pace, who was assisted by Mr Litt, the Chairman of the Shropshire Horticultural Society. The bridge cost in the region of £2,650, of which £2,000 was given by the Horticultural Society, with the remainder being raised by the residents of Porthill. The suspension bridge is 10ft wide and built of lattice steel. The ferry from the boathouse that had taken passengers across the river at this point for over 300 years was no longer needed. The crane is part of a major project to lay a water main across the river.

Water Lane, Frankwell, *c.* 1940. The photographer is looking across the natural ford over the River Severn towards Water Lane into Frankwell. It is believed that this was the way out of town before a bridge was erected. Even after the building of the weir in 1910 it is still possible in a dry summer for a man to cross at this point with the water not reaching much above his knees. The buildings on the riverside were removed in 2002 with the erection of the flood barrier. The long corrugated shed on the left was part of Ernie Welsby's scrap-iron yard. Mr Welsby traded there for many years and is remembered for being Mayor of Frankwell on several occasions. The buildings on the right are part of Birch's Skin Yard at the back of the Fellmongers Hall. The little building with the small windows on the right of the wall was where the men who worked there had their lunch breaks. Note the manhole in the river wall at the bottom of the lane that used to eject waste from the yard into the Severn, making this a good part of the river to fish for eels.

The River Severn, c. 1890. This is a view across the frozen river from the Quarry to Kingsland. On the left an area has been swept to allow skating and other winter activities. In the background are the steps down to the School's Ferry, which was redundant during this cold snap, and further up the river bank the Pengwern Boat Club. The boathouse was designed by J.L. Randal and was opened in 1881. It cost £1,000 and was paid for by a special fund that was set up to raise the money. In the foreground people are using the landing stage belonging to Richard Ellis to get on to the ice. During the summer months Mr Ellis hired out punts and racing, fishing and pleasure boats by the hour or by the day from this pontoon. He established the business in 1859 and was there for nearly fifty years until he sold his fleet of craft to George Cooper in 1906.

The River Severn, *c.* 1890. This view looking upstream was from the Kingsland Bridge, which had been completed by 1881 but not opened to traffic until the following year. There were several hard winters throughout the nineteenth century, the most memorable being a thirteen-week frost that lasted from December 1813 to March 1814, a ten-week frost that lasted over the same period between 1829 and 1830, an eight-week frost in 1839, a seven-week frost in 1855 and a big freeze of ten weeks that lasted from December 1878 to February 1879. The cold snap of 1881 was only a short one but cold enough to freeze the Severn to a degree that enabled skating on the river. Hundreds of skaters converged daily around Blockley's Hole near the Greyfriar's Bridge to enjoy the conditions. In the Quarry a large bonfire was built on the ice and as the evening advanced fireworks were lit and rockets fired to entertain the crowds. One group of people who did not enjoy a prolonged freeze were the ferry boat owners, who lost a great deal of trade when potential customers were able to walk across the river.

The School's Ferry, *c.* 1900. The oarsman poses in midstream by the ferry, just upstream of the Kingsland Bridge. The old lime trees are in the Quarry and St Chad's Church is on the right-hand side. A new boat ramp has been built on the Quarry side of the river, which was probably used by the ferry as well. Until January 1880, when the Greyfriars Bridge was opened, only three bridges spanned the Severn at Shrewsbury. They were the English and Welsh Bridges and the railway viaduct. For a direct route into town pedestrians had to rely on seven ferries stationed around the river. The first ferry upstream was between Smithfield Road and Frankwell; it was mainly used when sporting activities were taking place on the County Ground. The winding gear can still be seen on the Frankwell side. Next came the Boathouse ferry that was replaced by a bridge in 1922, and then Shrewsbury School's ferry that lasted until the 1930s and was used by the Prince of Wales when he visited the school in June 1932. Just below the Kingsland Bridge was the Cann Office ferry that ran between Coney Green and Crescent Lane between 1750 and 1896. Further downstream was Trouncer's ferry that crossed the river close to the Greyfriar's Bridge, Underdale ferry that ran from the bottom of Bradford Street to Castlefields and the Horse ferry at the bottom of Underdale Road.

The River Severn from Coney Green, *c.* 1917. This cold, murky winter's scene was taken during the early years of the twentieth century. The trees on the Quarry side of the river were planted in 1897, the year of Queen Victoria's Diamond Jubilee, when a new walk from Kingsland Bridge to St Julian's Friars was laid out and named Victoria Avenue. The chimney and the buildings in the centre are part of Lowcock's Foundry, most of which was demolished in about 1935. The foundry was established by William Hazledine who worked closely with Thomas Telford on a number of projects, including the building of the Menai Bridge. Later, the foundry was famous for producing the Lowcock Fuel Economiser, which heated the water to steam boilers using 20 per cent less coal. The chimney in the distance belongs to the Coleham pumping station.

The River Severn, *c.* 1890. This view is looking upstream to the Kingsland Bridge and to Richard Ellis's pontoon for hiring boats beneath the bridge. The Cann Office ferry gave access to the town from Kingsland via Coney Green on the left and Crescent Lane on the right. The ferry was in operation between 1750 and 1893. Two suggestions have been put forward for the name, the first that it had links with the Cann Office Hotel, just over the border in Wales; the second that Cann is similar to a Welsh word for white and as there was a linen-weaving factory nearby this area could have been used for the bleaching of the cloth. The ferry was owned by a Mr Johnson at the time of the Great Flood of 1795. As the waters rose a good deal of timber belonging to him was washed away, and as he and two men tried to salvage it their boat capsized. One man was drowned while the other swam ashore. Mr Johnson was pulled to shore by rescuers who unfortunately drowned him by holding him upside-down with his head under the water in the mistaken notion that this would get rid of all the water he had swallowed!

Carline Fields, *c.* 1940. The area was named after the Carline family of stonemasons who came to the town in the eighteenth century and were involved in many projects, including the erection of the English and Welsh Bridges, the Column, the houses on Claremont Bank and St Michael's Church. They lived in a house that stood on the site of the Wakeman School and their stone yard was Abbey Gardens where pieces of their work can still be seen. Carline Fields was made up of two rows of houses, one running off at a right angle to the other. One row consisted of twenty-three houses, while the other, known as Carline Terrace, had ten. The area was prone to flooding as the site was bordered by the River Severn and the Rea Brook. By the 1970s the area had been cleared and was used for several years as a car park and as a venue by travelling fairs and circuses. The site is now occupied by some handsome Georgian-style town houses that have been erected above the flood plain.

The English Bridge from the rear of the Royal Salop Infirmary, *c.* 1924. The bridge is built on the site of a natural ford that was created by sand, gravel and other debris being washed out of the Rea Brook, which joins the Severn at this point, to be deposited on the river bed. The islands are also created by these deposits. The Gay Meadow, the home of Shrewsbury Town Football Club, is just behind the trees on the opposite side of the river. Above the bridge to the left are the houses on Carline Fields. The large building to the right was built as a woollen mill by the Revd Edward Powis and a Mr Hodges. It was adapted into a cotton mill by Charles Hulbert and later into a brush factory. The building just to the right with the wide eaves is the Drill Hall, which was formally opened by Lord Bradford in 1881.

The English Bridge, 1925. This is the view of the bridge from downstream, before reconstruction was started. On the left is the Congregational church in Abbey Foregate. Carved on the keystone of the central arch is the head of Sabrina, the goddess of the River Severn. Above her are the arms of the town, three lions' or leopards' heads, known locally as the Logger Heads. Flanking the arch are two stone dolphins. Local tradition believes that when the Severn flows to the height of the dolphins' mouths, the water begins to rise up through the drains and into Abbey Foregate. Through the arch is the steam pile driver that would prepare the river bed for the supports of the temporary bridge that was built upstream of the old bridge. The first pile was driven on 28 May 1925.

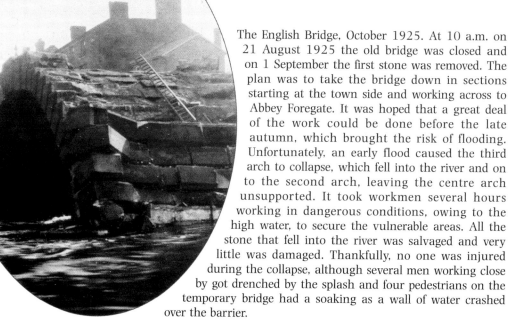

The English Bridge, October 1925. At 10 a.m. on 21 August 1925 the old bridge was closed and on 1 September the first stone was removed. The plan was to take the bridge down in sections starting at the town side and working across to Abbey Foregate. It was hoped that a great deal of the work could be done before the late autumn, which brought the risk of flooding. Unfortunately, an early flood caused the third arch to collapse, which fell into the river and on to the second arch, leaving the centre arch unsupported. It took workmen several hours working in dangerous conditions, owing to the high water, to secure the vulnerable areas. All the stone that fell into the river was salvaged and very little was damaged. Thankfully, no one was injured during the collapse, although several men working close by got drenched by the splash and four pedestrians on the temporary bridge had a soaking as a wall of water crashed over the barrier.

The English Bridge, 1926. In December 1921 a committee was set up to look into the reconstruction of the bridge and Arthur Ward the Borough Surveyor was given the task of drawing up the plans. He devised a scheme, which involved taking down the old bridge stone by stone, removing the hump in the middle, widening the carriageway and rebuilding it using as much of the old stonework as possible. In this way the town still had an elegant Georgian structure but without the old restrictions. Here the steelwork of a new arch is in place. Note the crane and the temporary bridge in the background. Before the temporary bridge was used it was tested by Sentinel steam wagons each loaded with over 12 tons of ballast. It was opened to pedestrians on 19 August 1925, the first day of the annual Flower Show.

The English Bridge, c. 1926. The photographer is looking towards Abbey Foregate. To the right are the Congregational Church and the tower of the Abbey. To the left of the end arch is John Carline's house, which was converted into a technical college in 1899. As the old bridge was dismantled the stone was stored in large piles in the Midland Yard in Abbey Foregate and were marked Arch A or Arch B, and so on, until the whole of the old bridge was there in pieces. The only sections of the old bridge not to be removed were strips of the two end arches; each 18ft wide after the facing stone was removed. Four electric cranes were erected downstream of the old structure. They were built above the flood plain and linked by wooden walkways. Each crane, which could hoist a weight of 3 tons, had a 100ft jib that could reach to the far side of the bridge and overlap with its neighbour when a larger stone was lifted.

Union Wharf, *c.* 1950. The large building on the top of the hill is the Royal Salop Infirmary. The hospital was opened on that site on 25 April 1747 in an old mansion called Broome Hall. This building was erected between 1828 and 1830 and cost in the region of £16,000. A large plot of land below the hospital was given to the Dominican friars who moved into the town in 1222. Two sons of Edward IV were born in the friary. The first was Prince Richard, Duke of York, who was murdered with his elder brother in the Tower of London; the second was Prince George who died in infancy. After the Battle of Shrewsbury in 1403 many of the higher-ranking dead were buried there. During excavations of the site in 1801 six skeletons were dug up. Five were normal, but the sixth was a giant measuring 7ft 2in. In 1823 the land by the river was leased to the Union Wharf Company. The building on the tow path was built as a warehouse but with the decline of waterborne trade it was used for a variety of purposes including the temporary housing of the Lancastrian School, a tavern and for many years by antique dealer G.R. Wycherly as workshops and for storage. In the 1970s it was tastefully renovated and converted into a pair of town houses by the De Saulle family.

St Mary's, Water Lane, *c.* 1890. This is the sole surviving gateway in the town's thirteenth-century defences. A second gate, known as St Mary's Gate, once stood at the top where the town wall crossed the lane. The lower Watergate is sometimes called Traitor's Gate, as it is said that a Parliamentary sympathiser unlocked the gates during the night of 21 February 1645 to aid the Roundheads to capture the town from the Royalists. In the past the lane has been known as Frerelode, St Mary's Waturlode and Marwell Street.

The railway viaduct, c. 1900. The photographer is standing on the Gay Meadow side of the river. The castle wall and the base of Laura's Tower are top left while the station and the viaduct are middle right. The first stone of the viaduct was laid on 31 August 1847 and it was completed before the opening of the Shrewsbury to Birmingham Railway in June 1849. It has seven elliptical arches, each with a 45ft span. It was built out of Broseley brick with Grinshill stone dressing and piers. Between 1899 and 1902 two iron extensions were added on either side of the original bridge by the Cleveland Iron Company, to cope with extra traffic using the station. The original viaduct carried three tracks over the river, but the new extension made it possible to increase this to nine as well as developing the station over the river with the addition of seven platforms. Work was hindered during the flood of 1899. Huge crowds gathered outside the prison to see if the wooden structure erected by the company could withstand the huge pressure of water and although completely submerged it remained intact. Note the side of the Severn Junction signal-box, top right, that used to straddle the old bridge and the steam pile drivers that prepared the river bed for the huge ornamental columns that would support the viaduct.

Across the river to the castle, *c*. 1930. Dominating the view is Shrewsbury Castle. The original motte and bailey castle was built on the site of Laura's Tower by Roger de Montgomery shortly after the Norman Conquest. Laura's Tower (left) was built by Thomas Telford when he was turning the castle into a home in 1787 for Sir William Poultney who was MP for Shrewsbury. The castle was added to and altered many times over the years. The rounded towers to the right were added between 1280 and 1300 during the reign of Edward I. Below the castle is the massive glass and iron roof of the railway station, which was dismantled in the early 1960s when it was found to be unsafe. To the right is Shrewsbury Prison, which was erected between 1787 and 1793 at a cost of about £30,000. The initial design was by Haycock, but this was modified by Telford, who is also credited with designing the imposing entrance with its bust of John Howard (1726–90), the great prison reformer, over the gates. The house below the station stands on the site of Aenon Cottage, named after a Baptist minister who lived there. He used to baptise his converts on the Castle Ford in the Severn below his house. The ford disappeared when the new weir was built, which raised the height of the river at this point by several feet.

The Weir, Castlefields, *c*. 1950. At the beginning of the twentieth century, with new sewers emptying into the Severn, the state of the river around the town especially in hot dry summers was becoming intolerable. The growing sport of rowing was also affected as in low water it was almost impossible to take a boat past the fords at the English or Welsh Bridges. This site was chosen on which to build the weir that would maintain a minimum level of water throughout the year. While preparing the river bed the remains of an old barge was found and hauled up on to the bank on the Underdale side for people to inspect. The work on the 195ft weir was carried out between 1910 and 1912. It had a boat pass which allowed rowers to travel downstream, but over the years it fell into disrepair. The fisherman is standing on the remains of the old pass, the loss of which has caused many disputes between boat users and the authorities.

4

The Beautiful Quarry &
The World's Wonder Show

Quarry Lodge, c. 1900. The Quarry Lodge was erected in 1886 after the Shropshire Horticultural Society had made a donation of £486 6s 5d from the Flower Show profits. For many years it was the home of Shrewsbury's park superintendent, the most famous being Percy Thrower, Britain's head gardener. He became a household institution, bringing the joys of gardening to the people through his radio and television programmes and the many books he wrote on the subject. After he moved to a new home at Bomere Heath the council allowed the society to use the lodge as offices at a peppercorn rent. Other donations given by the society towards beautifying the town included £216 in 1881 for the erection of the ornamental gates to the right of the lodge and £500 18s 7d for improvements to St Chad's Terrace, which included replacing the wall behind the children. The end of St Chad's unusual round nave is on the right.

The Quarry, *c.* 1890. Children enjoy the winter weather by tobogganing down Central Avenue, now Gloucester Avenue. On the right is Quarry Lodge. The large block of houses on the left is known as Claremont Buildings. It dates from the late eighteenth century and was built by John Carline. Nos 2 to 4 were once the Claremont School for Ladies run by Mrs and Miss Wood. In an advert they advised parents of prospective pupils that the school was in the best position in Shrewsbury, overlooking the Quarry and that all pupils would receive 'a thorough Education in all branches of study, and are entered for all Local Examinations, also for the Royal Academy of Music and the School of Science and Art'.

The Dingle, *c.* 1895. Two young lads pose on their toboggan for the photographer on the gentle slope leading to the centre of the formal gardens. The photographer is looking in the direction of the Eye, Ear and Throat Hospital; the slope to the right of the statue is now occupied by the rockery. The Dingle was first landscaped in 1879, the same year that the statue of Sabrina, by Birmingham sculptor Peter Hollins, was presented to the town by a former Earl of Bradford. From this position she was moved on to the bank looking across the Dingle to the bandstand and in 1985 to a location at the end of the ornamental pond, where she has become part of an attractive water feature.

Opposite, botton: Central Avenue in the Quarry, *c.* 1900. A statue of Hercules was placed at the bottom of the avenue on the banks of the Severn in 1881. This was because his original position at the top of the avenue was needed for the erection of new ornamental gates leading into the Quarry. Local legend reports that the avenues of trees were planted in one night by Thomas Wright, two friends and the help of magic. However, this short minute recorded by the Corporation and dated 15 January 1719 is nearer the truth: 'Agreed that there be a handsome walk made in the Quarry for persons to walk in and that trees be planted in the same manner as Mr Mayor shall think most ornamental.' The total cost for the work was £65 14s, which was thought to have been paid by the Mayor, Henry Jenks. In 1974 Central Avenue was renamed Gloucester Avenue after Princess Alice, Duchess of Gloucester, who graced the Flower Show with her presence that year.

The Dingle, *c.* 1890. Children gather on the frozen pond in the Dingle for some winter sport. The building in the background is the Hatchery, which is surrounded by the lime trees that were thinned out as more of the Dingle was landscaped. Skating on ponds was thought to be safer than on rivers and during this winter pools at Springfield, Sutton, Bomere and Alkmund Park were used as well as sections of the old canal.

The Dingle, *c.* 1910. This view looks across the pond to the Hatchery on the left and the Shoemaker's Arbour in the centre. The scene at the rear is dominated by the old lime trees that were chopped down in the late 1940s. The entrance to the Shoemaker's Arbour was moved to the Dingle in June 1880. It was erected on Kingsland in 1679 at a cost of £28 6s 7d. The hall that it fronted was octagonal in shape and built with a timber frame and lattice wood. Next to the arbour was a maze known as The Shoemaker's Race, which contained a walk of a measured mile within an area of a few square yards. The Hatchery occupied that position for many years until it was removed in the 1980s when that end of the pond was remodelled. It was once used by the Shrewsbury Angling Club to hatch and rear salmon to release into the Severn.

The Dingle, *c.* 1900. At the rear against the backdrop of the old lime trees is the Hatchery. The arch of the Shoemaker's Arbour is visible to the right of the couple sitting on the bench in front of the pond. To the extreme right is a large chestnut tree, the last of several that once occupied this area. The others were destroyed after the pond had been dredged and the mud removed, which was piled around their bases. The surviving tree had a circular bench built around its trunk, where visitors could sit in the shade and enjoy the view across the formal flower beds. Unfortunately, it was knocked to the ground by a fierce gale that created havoc in the county in April 1947. The fountain in the centre was given to the town in 1889 by the Independent Order of Oddfellows.

The Dingle, 23 May 1933. Princess Mary the Princess Royal was the daughter of King George V and Queen Mary. She was a regular visitor to the town and on this occasion had a very busy schedule. The main reason for her visit was to open the new 4½-mile Shrewsbury bypass between Shelton and Emstry that would ease traffic problems in the centre of town. She also visited a number of hospitals and attended the Empire Day celebrations in the Quarry. The Princess is inspecting the Dingle on her way to the bandstand where the schoolchildren were gathered to sing patriotic songs. She is being escorted by the Mayor, Richard Mansell, and Chief Constable Frank Davies of the Borough police force. The Dingle was described as 'a blaze of colour', the paths lined 'with small school girls, each prettily dressed in a delicate coloured frock and wearing a green petal-shaped cap. The children carried flower baskets and as the Princess passed, each one made a little curtsy.'

Opposite, bottom: The Flower Show, *c.* 1924. Vast crowds gather around the main arena to witness the show jumping, another of the show's great attractions. It was introduced to the programme of events in 1891 when it was known as horse leaping. Prize money in those early years was generous with first place receiving £20, second £10 and third £5. In 1924 thirty-four competitors competed from as far afield as Penrith, Berkhamsted and Bristol. As well as horse leaping Yeomanry competitions also took place in the main arena, which included tent pegging and the apple and bucket race. One of the favourite competitors in the 1920s was Sergeant Major Harold Whitfield of 'H' Squadron of the Shropshire Yeomanry whose bravery in the First World War won him the Victoria Cross. During the 1950s and '60s most of Britain's greatest international jumpers graced the Quarry, including Colonel Harry Llewellyn, Pat Smythe, Harvey Smith and David Broome.

The Quarry, August 1952. This view of the Quarry and the Flower Show was taken from Kingsland. As the evening draws, in the bandstand, Porthill Bridge and the main walks are all illuminated with hundreds of coloured lights. At first the newly planted trees were not tall enough to take the rows of lights, so flag poles had to be erected in between to do the job. The previous year the Horticultural Society played a big part in the creation of an English Garden in Berlin. The son of the society's Chairman, Wing Commander Michael Everest, was stationed in Berlin and became involved when he heard that the commanding officer, General Bourne, wanted to create the garden to mark the growing trust and friendship between the English and German people. Percy Thrower was despatched to Berlin to draw up plans, which were approved by the society, and a donation of £93 2s 11d was given towards the cost. Plants and shrubs were also donated from nurseries and gardens from all over the country, including a gift from George VI and Queen Elizabeth from their garden at Windsor.

The Flower Show, *c.* 1925. This view was taken from the stage and shows the huge crowds who would sit all day to be entertained by music hall and circus acts from all over the world. In 1893 spectators were guaranteed eight hours of entertainment by some of the most wonderful artists in the world with a fresh performance every fifteen minutes. Acts included the Wichman Brothers on the tightrope, trapeze artists Lolo, Sylvester and Lola and the Three Ottos in Fun and Mischief. In 1924 the *Chronicle* announced the stage entertainment was 'unrivalled' as 'the world's finest gymnasts and acrobats are gathered together in the Quarry each year and their feats of strength and daring are wondrous indeed, whirlwind action and snappy comedy combine in holding the attention of the vast crowd'. The stage acts went out of fashion and were abandoned in the 1960s when the public could watch a number of variety shows on television in the comfort of their own homes.

The Flower Show, *c.* 1925. The spellbinding high-wire acts were first introduced to the show in 1880. They were soon established as a firm favourite with the crowds and hundreds of spectators would be drawn to witness feats of outstanding skill, which left them breathless. One commentator at the time observed that 'One of the secrets of the amazing popularity of the Shrewsbury Floral Fête is the fact that all classes, all social grades and all interests are abundantly catered for. It embraces in its appeal all the best features of a flower show, a gigantic vaudeville show and throws in the whole gamut of attractions usually only to be found at such famous amusement centres as Belle Vue Manchester or Crystal Palace.'

The Flower Show, *c.* 1901. An intrepid photographer risks life and limb to secure this superb view of the showground in the Quarry. At this date Percival and Arthur Spencer, who were known as The Crystal Palace Aeronauts, offered visitors to the show special captive flights in one of their balloons for just 5*d*. Between 2 p.m. and 7 p.m. a constant stream of visitors enjoyed the experience of being launched up to 500ft into the air at the end of a long rope. The brothers also entertained the crowds by doing two free ascents from the Quarry on both days. In this view the photographer has caught the crowds gathered around the bandstand, which was the Horticultural Society's second gift to the town. It was erected in 1879 and cost £233 5*s* 2*d*.

5

How We Used to Shop

The Corner of Meadow Place and Castle Gates, *c.* 1891. The two men are standing at the door of a provisions shop that in 1886 was owned by Jones and Griffith. The firm also had two warehouses in Meadow Place, one just below their shop and another at the bottom of the bank near Smithfield Road. In a local directory they advertised 'Jones and Griffith Wholesale Grocers, Importers of American Produce. Shoppers will do well to Visit this Establishment when Buying. ONLY FIRST-CLASS GOODS. Sold at Lowest Market Prices.' By 1891 the business was being run by William J. Griffith. However, by 1896 the shop had closed and was occupied by a furnishing depot belonging to F.W. Harper, who had also taken over the warehouse next to the shop and converted it into a temperance hotel. The shop was later converted into James Baker's shoe shop before the whole corner was demolished to make way for the Granada Cinema.

Castle Street, *c.* 1938. The new shop frontage of WHSmith can be seen on the right. The road between Smith's and the restaurant is School Gardens. It was once known as Rotton or Ratten Lane, which led to the old County Gaol, Shrewsbury School and through to Castle Gates. The lane was closed as a through road in about 1826. Pailin's cake shop in the lane was established in 1760 and was used for many years by the boys of Shrewsbury School as a tuck shop. It was also the home of the famous Shrewsbury Cake. Thomas Plimmer, who had worked for the firm from the age of fourteen, purchased the business in the 1870s and continued to make Shrewsbury Cake. He also established a restaurant capable of accommodating 200 people and was widely known as a general caterer who was regularly engaged by the top families in the county to provide dinners for a variety of functions. Soon after this photograph was taken the shop was dismantled and rebuilt several feet further back from the road. The building next door housed Lennard's shoe shop. Before that the top section of the building was a ladies' clothes shop known as the Ark, while the other half was the Talbot Inn.

Opposite: Castle Street, *c.* 1886. These buildings stand almost opposite School Lane. The two timber-framed houses are very similar in style and date from the sixteenth century. They were erected as two-storey buildings, the third storey added at a later date as an extension. The house on the left belonged to G.H. Jones, a tobacconist, who advertised in 1886 that he sold every brand of foreign cigars of the 1885 crop. The business was taken over by Singleton and Cole who had a large cigarette and cigar factory in Hill's Lane, and then by Arthur Bolton, whose family continued to run it until the 1950s. The house on the right was occupied by the plumbing firm of Evans and Morris. By 1891 the business had been acquired by Scull Brothers who advertised as 'Sanitary Specialists, Plumbing, Heating, and Ventilating Engineers'. The old building has been replaced by a late Victorian timber-framed house. The building in the middle was a private house at this time and occupied by the two Price sisters. By 1900 it was converted into a piano shop by Richard Price and later into a hairdresser's run by William Edwards.

Castle Street, *c.* 1934 and *c.* 1946. For many years this double-fronted Georgian building, dating from 1723, was the shop and studio occupied by two Shrewsbury photographers, first by John Laing, who was there from 1863 to about 1900, then by Richard Bartlett. Local historians are grateful to both photographers, who did a great deal to record early images of the town. When the two photographs are compared it is noticeable that the building has an extra storey on the older one. The top storey was added to make a studio and was constructed out of glass about 5ft in height to allow in the maximum amount of light to expose photographic plates. In the early 1930s the shop was occupied by Esther Hardwick, a ladies' outfitters. The building was altered when the District Bank, under the management of Mr G.C.C. Atkinson, opened a branch in part of the building in 1935. By 1972 the bank had been taken over by the National Westminster, which extended its business into the photographic shop of R.G. Lewis. For a short time Esther Hardwick had run her shop from the premises later occupied by R.G. Lewis.

Opposite: Pride Hill, *c.* 1886. William Francis Watkins poses proudly outside his tailor's shop on Pride Hill. He started working with his father in Claremont Street in the 1860s, eventually taking the business over before moving to Pride Hill. In 1900 he advertised that the firm had been established in 1846. His shop specialised in making servants' livery of all kinds, hunting breeches in the newest styles, and it gave special attention to clerical outfits. He was the sole agent in Shrewsbury and the district for Burberry's gabardine specialities. William's son went into business with him and continued to run the shop until the mid-1920s when the premises was occupied by Manfield & Sons Ltd, the boot and shoemakers. The shop to the left was occupied by Jonathan Coleman, a hosier, who was also the landlord of the Royal Vaults on Wyle Cop; while to the right was a draper and silk mercer's shop belonging to E. Birch Legh & Company.

Pride Hill, *c.* 1945. Although there are still fragments of timber-framed buildings behind some of the frontages in Pride Hill, this is the last to survive in its entirety. The building was erected as a two-storey house in the early part of the sixteenth century with the central three-storeyed gable being added around a century later when more space was needed. The front is attractively decorated with different motifs including the familiar quatrefoil and an unusual pattern of dragons over the modern shop window. The balustrade either side of the gable on the first floor is a much later addition. The building has been used for a number of businesses. In the 1870s and 1880s it was a tobacconist's shop owned by William Rheece. By 1896 James Page had opened a clothes shop there, which later traded under the name of the Cash Clothing Company. The shop was occupied in 1917 by Mrs M. Groves who was selling fruit, but by 1922 she had changed her business and was listed as a Fancy Repository. From the end of the 1920s until the 1980s it reverted back to a tobacconist's run first by Pelican & Snelson and then by A. Preedy & Sons. In 1903 Pelican & Snelson was the 'Originator and Sole Proprietor of "The Celebrated Shropshire Hunt" Smoking Mixture and Cigarettes'. Today Thornton's sells its delicious chocolates from there.

The Abbot's House, Butcher Row, *c.* 1905. The Abbot's House stands on the corner of Butcher Row and Fish Street. The house dates from 1459 and was built on land belonging to Lilleshall Abbey. It is recorded that at a ceremony attended by the abbot and held on the site in April of that year, that 20*d* was given to the abbot's carpenter as a reward for his work and 14*d* was spent on wine. Along the frontage in Butcher Row are a set of medieval windows and a large entrance leading to the rear of the house. The premises on the corner is occupied by Henry Harper, a basket maker, who is displaying his wares outside his shop. To the right were the offices of a local building firm, Jones & Son, the sign of which is hanging on the side of the building. Next door was the home of Mrs Sarah Griffith, who let out part of her house as apartments.

Opposite: The building at the top of Butcher Row and the narrow road between Butcher Row and St Alkmund's Place, *c.* 1938. The passage to the left of the door is the entrance into the Burial Shut leading through to St Alkmund's graveyard. The building was occupied by Shuker's Central Garage from 1896 until about 1918 when it was used by Foulkes, Wales & Company Ltd, automobile engineers. John Blower was part of J. & B. Blower Ltd, house furnishers, removal and storage contractors, house agents and funeral directors, which had premises on Pride Hill and Castle Gates. In 1914 the firm had been responsible for furnishing the Royal Pavilion for King George V at the Royal Agricultural Show held on the Racecourse at Monkmoor. At the end of the 1930s a mammoth sale was held as the lease was expiring. The large posters in the window announce to passersby that 'All Stock Must Be Disposed Of At Greatly Reduced Prices' and that 'No Reasonable Offer Will Be Refused For Quick Disposal Of Oddments'. Note Commandant, the prize bull, painted by Edwin Cole, hanging outside the Bull Inn. The ladies with the pram are standing outside Mansfield's butcher's shop. Just beyond is Smith's Temperance Hotel and John Barton's dairy. This corner is now occupied by the main entrance to the Prince Rupert Hotel.

Wyle Cop, *c.* 1914. The timber-framed building on the right is known as Henry Tudor House, as he is believed to have lodged there in August 1485 enroute to the Battle of Bosworth. The house dates from 1430 and was once the home of the Elisha family, who gave their name to the passageway to the right until it was changed to Barracks Passage. The fine tracery window on the second floor was discovered under plaster in about 1910. Harry Mudd, the Grimsby fishmonger, took the business over from William Roberts in about 1893 and was there until the 1940s. The draper's shop to the left is housed in the old Compasses Inn and was run by Joseph Cooper. The business was bought by Maurice Davey who extended his shop into Mudd's when the fishmonger closed down.

Wyle Cop, *c.* 1890. Vincent Corbett Legh Crump had two confectionery shops, here on Wyle Cop and another at 1 St Mary's Street. Like Thomas Plimmer in Castle Street he was able to supply the people of the town with the famous Shrewsbury Cake that had been presented to Princess Victoria when she visited in 1832. Never one to hide his light under a bushel, Mr Crump reminds customers of the royal connection with his advert for the cakes and the royal warrant over the front of his shop. As well as running two shops he was also involved in a number of other activities. He was financial clerk to the council and secretary to the Music Hall Company Ltd, the Pengwern Boat Club and the Permanent Benefit Building Society in the Square. In 1886 he lived in Belle Vue Road, but by 1900 had moved to Crescent Place, Town Walls. The shop to the right was known as the Berlin Wool Shop and Fancy Repository, which was run by his sister Louisa Jane Crump.

High Street, *c.* 1925. Workmen are repairing the awning over the front of Murrell's shop on the corner of High Street and Grope Lane. Edwin Murrell was a nurseryman, seedsman and florist who acquired the business from Oldroyd & Company in about 1880. They had a large garden centre at Portland Nurseries near the Column and a shop at the Fish Street end of High Street before moving to these premises in about 1905. From the balcony Benjamin Disraeli addressed the people of Shrewsbury in 1841 when he stood as the town's MP. Although he was elected, few of his supporters were at this rally and he was pelted with rotten eggs and vegetables. On the other corner of Grope Lane is the gentlemen's outfitter's run by Thomas Golling. It was formerly an inn called the Cross Keys, occupied in the early nineteenth century by the Stanton family. To supplement their income John Stanton Snr ran a gunsmith's there while his son sold toys, jewellery and cutlery. Next door is the shop of Alberta Batsford who sold ladies' wear and was known as the Blouse Specialist.

The Square, *c.* 1880. These buildings are situated on the west side of the Square between Market Street to the left and the Gullet Passage to the right. In 1896 the firm of Adnitt & Naunton claimed it had been established for over 200 years. It traded as a bookseller, stationer, printer, lithographer and bookbinder. It had the largest stock of books in Shropshire, with presentation volumes in elegant bindings. It sold leather goods, artists' materials and a full range of photographic equipment, as well as photographs of Shrewsbury and the neighbourhood taken by all the principal photographers. Both Mr Adnitt and Mr Naunton were founder members of Shrewsbury Flower Show and were joint secretaries from 1875 to 1912. Mr Adnitt was also the Borough Auditor and secretary of the Shropshire Country Club, while Mr Naunton was secretary for the Kingsland Bridge Company, the Shropshire Electric Light and Power Company and the Shropshire Camera Club. Next door is the office of *Eddowes's Salopian Journal*, a local newspaper that was published every Wednesday. The paper had a strong Conservative bias while its great rival the *Shrewsbury Chronicle* was staunchly Liberal.

Mardol, *c.* 1905. This is the fine timber-framed house on the corner of Mardol and Hill's Lane. It dates from about 1620 but was completely renovated in 1988 when the frontage was restored to its original shape. At the turn of the twentieth century the building was still divided into two shops. The one on the right was occupied by Richard Giles, a watch and clock maker. The shop was later used by Clement Allcock who also had another business outlet on Pride Hill. Edward Birch had the shop next door for about fifty years. He was a hairdresser, umbrella and sunshade manufacturer and tobacconist, importing Havana cigars and tobacco. His motto was 'Never Too Late To Mend' and he advertised 'Repairs Neatly Executed'.

6

Outside the Bridges

Coleham Head to Abbey Foregate, *c*. 1910. The house in the centre was built by John Carline, a stonemason who came to Shrewsbury in the eighteenth century. It was a private house until the late 1880s when it was occupied by Mrs Palin. The house was converted into a boarding and day school by William Tutton before it became Shrewsbury Technical College in 1899. The college housed technical and commercial classes, a school of art and a centre for training pupil teachers. The building was demolished in 1935 and the present Wakeman School built in its place. The building on the right is the Swan Inn, which had stood on the site since the seventeenth century. The inn was owned by Soames's Brewery and had seven private and four public rooms with accommodation for nine people and stabling for six horses.
The customers were well behaved although in August 1898 the landlord was fined £2 plus costs for allowing gaming to take place on the premises. Just above the inn are the lights at the entrance to the Congregational church. The English Bridge is to the left.

Abbey Foregate, December 1869. The waters of the River Severn began to ooze out of the drain near the buildings behind the railings on the far side of the Foregate just five days before Christmas. The river rose to a height of 19ft 4in above summer level and over a foot of water entered the abbey church. It was the highest flood since the great flood of 1795, which was over a foot higher. People passing over the English and Welsh Bridges during the 1869 flood were alarmed by the shaking of the bridges and by the noise of the water passing beneath, which sounded like the roar of thunder. Note the railway bridge on the left, which is completely boxed in. When first erected it was open sided, but the noise of the steam engines caused so many horses to bolt up the Foregate that the authorities enclosed it.

Abbey Foregate, *c.* 1881. This view of the abbey was taken before the east end was rebuilt and the roof line had been restored to its original height. The date is uncertain, but their were four floods in 1880 ranging in height from 18ft to 16ft 10in. This is probably the flood of February 1881, as it reached a height of 18ft 10in and would have surrounded the church as this one has done. A report stated that 'The water first appeared on the left hand side of the road, which was covered on Friday morning. Standing still until late in the evening the volume began to increase about ten o'clock at night, and by Saturday had entirely covered both roads, the water then pouring out of the Abbey Mill in a rapid stream, consequent upon the overflow of the Rea. The entire road at this point was under water, the stream reaching up to the abbey railings. Many houses in this part on the side nearest the river were surrounded by at least 18 inches of water causing the unenviable occupants to take refuge in the upper rooms, food and other things being handed in at the bedroom window from a raft.'

Coleham Head, January 1899. A boy watches intently as two men measure the depth of the floodwater outside Irt Villa. The benches and some seating from the Congregational church were used as a makeshift walk on the right between the English Bridge and the Rea Brook Bridge in the distance. The Coleham area was hit badly by this flood with all work being stopped at the Midland Carriage Works, Lowcock's Foundry, the Brush Factory and the new pumping station. The large building that stood by the entrance to Carline Fields on the right was occupied by grocer William Harris, chemist Charles Eldred, Frank Wheeler, a dried fish dealer, and shopkeeper John Jones. The row of houses on the left with the board advertising the provision of ale is Reabrooke Place. The small lean-to below was a fibrous plaster works owned by J. Wellings. By 1916 it had been converted into a garage and was known in 1922 as the Central Garage. In about 1931 J.R. Morris moved his Shrewsbury Circular Printing and Publishing Company from the centre of town to this location.

Abbey Foregate, *c.* 1937. This view was taken from the top of the abbey tower looking back towards the English Bridge. The cyclists are travelling towards town by the old road, while Telford's new road, which was put through the abbey precincts, is on the left. Apart from the abbey, Curton's garage and the cottages to the right are the oldest properties in the Foregate. They are cruck-framed with parts dating from 1408. The building surrounded by scaffolding is the new toilet block built on the site of Woodnorth's grocery shop. The frontage was constructed from timber rescued from the buildings demolished in Barker Street. To the left is Rowland's fruit shop and Halford's café. The white building with the large sign over the front elevation is the Bull Inn. Its most famous landlord was Edward Edwards, known to his friends and customers as Double Ned. At his housewarming party in 1843, a spacious pavilion was erected at the rear to accommodate 383 guests. Dinner commenced at 4 p.m. and they were treated to 'a sumptuous meal consisting of prime venison and every other dainty that could possibly be procured'.

Lord Hill's Column, *c*. 1918. It was erected to celebrate the achievements of Shropshire's greatest soldier, Rowland Hill. He was one of Wellington's commanders during the Peninsular Wars and at the Battle of Waterloo. After the Iron Duke went into politics, Lord Hill replaced him as head of the British Army. The road directly behind the column is Preston Street, an ancient track leading to Weir Hill and Preston Boats. It has also been known as Brick-Kiln Lane as it leads to Clayhill where it is believed that bricks were made and fired. It was also known as Pack-Horse Lane as goods ferried across the river at Preston Boats were brought into town by horse-drawn transport along there. The roads forking to the right are the London and Wenlock roads. The site to the left of the column with the small caretaker's lodge is now occupied by the Shirehall and the fields beyond have all been built over at various times since the 1930s.

Preston Street, *c*. 1935. This view of the rear of Lord Hill's Column was taken from Preston Street. The turning on the right leads into gardens where the magistrates' court is now situated. In 1946 Sir Percy Thomas presented plans, which would have brought all the council offices, a hospital for 1,000 patients, emergency services, car park and recreational facilities into this area with the Column as the focal point. The plans were never implemented, and although the ambulance depot and the new Shirehall were built close by, neither were to Sir Percy's design. The idea for it was put forward by the owner of the *Shrewsbury Chronicle* on 17 December 1813, and the very next day at a meeting in the paper's newsroom on St John's Hill nearly £400 was donated towards the project. A year later, on 27 December 1814, the foundation stone was laid. In a cavity under the stone a bottle containing gold and silver coins of George III and a copy of the *Shrewsbury Chronicle* were placed.

Right and below: Whitehall, Monkmoor Road, *c.* 1925. This Elizabethan mansion was erected on the site of the monastic grange of Shrewsbury Abbey in 1578 by Richard Prynce, a lawyer. The stone used in its erection is thought to have come from the abbey buildings after the Dissolution. According to local legend the stone was whitewashed to conceal where it came from, but in fact it was quite common at that time to paint the porous sandstone to protect it from the elements and stop erosion. The gatehouse was added in 1582 to house the gatekeeper and chaplain. The turret on the top of the building is known as a Belvedere, a corruption of an Italian word for a place with a fine view. Later the hall was owned by the Earl of Tankerville before it was bought by Dr Samuel Butler, headmaster of Shrewsbury School and Bishop of Lichfield. The property was passed down

to his grandson Samuel, an author, who lived at Clifford's Inn, London. In 1886 he sold land to the north and east of the mansion for building. By 1900 it was owned by John Butler-Lloyd, the great-grandson of the bishop. In the 1920s it became a small hotel and country club run by Colonel Dugdale and Mr Ward. In recent years it has been used as offices before being converted into apartments in 2004/5. A few years earlier plans had been submitted to knock down the boundary wall between the gatehouse and King Street and erect houses on the site. Thankfully this act of vandalism was rejected.

Monkmoor, *c.* 1935. This wonderful aerial view shows practically the whole area from Abbey Foregate at the bottom to the River Severn at the top. Monkmoor Road is on the left. Towards the top of the road is Judith Butts, built by the council in the mid-1920s and opposite are the houses on Abbot's Road. At the very top are the large Belfast hangers belonging to Monkmoor Aerodrome. The first large-scale development took place in the area on the left-hand side of Monkmoor Road in 1854. Land around Orchard House was bought by the Shrewsbury Permanent Freehold Land and Building Society, shares were sold and the members were allocated land by ballot. A road was built through linking Monkmoor Road and Underdale Road; it was first called Union Street, but later changed to Bradford Street after one of the aristocratic families linked with the town. Cleveland Street and Tankerville Street were also named in the same way. The second piece of development took place around Whitehall at the bottom of the photograph towards the end of the nineteenth century. Part of the Whitehall estate was sold by Samuel Butler who named the new roads Bishop Street and Canon Street in memory of his grandfather and father, Clifford Street after his London home at Clifford's Inn, Fleet Street, and Alfred Street in recognition of his faithful valet, Alfred Cathie. King Street at the very bottom of the view was built between 1912 and 1914. The third major housing project known as the Racecourse Estate was built in the 1920s. It can be seen in the centre on part of the old racecourse. To help cover the cost of the new estate a strip of land along the right-hand side of Monkmoor Road was sold for private housing. The new estate incorporated all the best features of a garden city on similar lines to Port Sunlight, giving low-density housing and large open spaces. The estate was set out on two roads: Racecourse Avenue, which ran from Monkmoor Road up to Monkmoor School, and Racecourse Crescent, which curves in front of the school from Monkmoor Road to Crowmoor Road. The school opened in 1930 and was a major part of the landscape with its large gabled hall dominating the view along the avenue. The houses at the bottom of the avenue were also built at an angle to give the impression that they were lodges at the entrance to a grand estate.

Monkmoor Road, *c.* 1910. The moor belonged to Uffington parish but was transferred to Shrewsbury Abbey by Helgot, the principal landowner in Uffington at the time of the Domesday survey. The road was important as it was a direct route from Shrewsbury Abbey to Haughmond Abbey via the ferry at Uffington. In 1900 the road was in two parts: the first section from Abbey Foregate to Whitehall Street was called Monkmoor Street, while the road from Whitehall to the ferry was known as Monkmoor Road. As buildings were erected Monkmoor Street was extended, but by the middle of the 1920s the whole thoroughfare from Abbey Foregate was known as Monkmoor Road. Over the centuries the area has been put to many uses, but mainly farming; Monkmoor Farm is mentioned in deeds as early as 1545. In the nineteenth century a large area to the south was used as a racecourse. Monkmoor Hall was built as a grand residence but later used as an isolation hospital before it was demolished in the 1950s. An airfield was built in the area, which was used as a training school for aerial photography during the First World War and as an aircraft salvage depot during the Second. The unique Belfast hangars are now part of an industrial estate. At the beginning of the twentieth century a sewage works was opened at the top of the road on the banks of the river.

Monkmoor Aerodrome, October 1913. Land at the top end of Monkmoor was used as an airfield before the First World War. In October 1913 Gustav Hamel visited the town with his aeroplane and delighted a huge crowd with an extremely thrilling flying exhibition. He was only twenty-four at the time and was the son of Dr Gustav Hamel who had been the physician of King Edward VII. He taught himself to fly at Blériot's flying school in France in January 1911. In April 1912 he carried the first woman, Miss Trehawke Davies, across the Channel in his aircraft. He had also crossed the Channel fourteen times and reached a speed of 125mph. During the last months of the First World War the airfield was used as an Aircraft Acceptance Park and as an Observer School of Reconnaissance and Aerial Photography. During the Second World War it was used by the RAF as No. 34 Salvage Centre.

Haughmond Hill, c. 1900. Two unidentified ladies pose in front of the castle at the summit. The castle was a folly and was erected in about 1790 as a hunting lodge for the Corbet family who lived close by at Sundorne Castle. Unfortunately, the castle fell into disrepair and was allowed to collapse during the first half of the twentieth century. The name Haughmond is derived from the hill where the haws, the fruit of the hawthorn tree, grow. Before cheap-day excursions were available scores of people would walk along the old canal path or cross the river by ferry at Uffington, climb the hill and picnic on the summit on Good Fridays and bank holidays. Just below the summit was Nancy Spragg's cottage, which has since fallen down, where ramblers could purchase a cool glass of homemade lemonade and other refreshments.

Sundorne Castle, *c.* 1930. Sundorne Castle stood to the north-east of Shrewsbury and was occupied for many years by members of the Corbet family. It was designed by George Wyatt at the beginning of the nineteenth century, but there was evidence of a much older Georgian house that stood on the site. Within the house was a fine staircase, which dated from about 1740. There were also three fine stained-glass windows by Francis Eginton of Handsworth who created the beautiful east window in St Alkmund's Church. After the death of Annabelle, Lady Boughey, in May 1914 the contents of the house were auctioned at a seven-day sale by Hampton & Sons of Cockspur Street, London. The catalogue of the sale gives us an idea of how the castle was furnished. The furniture was principally of the old English type, there was some fine statuary including a Chantry bust, a Jacobean refectory table, antique French and English clocks, old lacquered cabinets and a cellar of choice wine. One of the important features of the sale was the library that contained over 3,000 volumes covering a variety of subjects and in the most expensive bindings. In March 1955 the trustees of the estate applied for permission to demolish the castle. No objection was raised, and although it was a building of great historical and architectural importance it was knocked down in September 1955. A brick gatehouse and part of a castellated wall survive and are thought to date from the Georgian period or a little earlier.

Little Harlescott Lane, *c.* 1910. Until the 1920s Harlescott was a small village on the outskirts of Shrewsbury, and Little Harlescott Lane a narrow country road linking Whitchurch Road to the Ellesmere Road. This changed after Hall Engineering Company bought land in the area to move the Chatwood Safe Company from Bolton. They also built a garden village opposite their new factory, which consisted of forty-four houses built to a high specification, with large gardens and sporting facilities close by. For thirty years the residents lived in peace and tranquillity in the Shropshire countryside until the area was swallowed up in the 1950s and '60s as Shrewsbury expanded. The lane is now an important artery in the town's road system.

Chester Street, January 1899. On Saturday 29 January the river rose at an alarming rate, with water being forced up drains, quickly filling cellars and inundating the ground floors of buildings in the lower parts of the town. So deep and fast flowing was the water that a walkway erected from Smithfield Road, down Chester Street to Coton Hill was washed away. Wagons and small traps were brought in to ferry people across with drivers charging the extortionate sum of 18*d* for the 300yd journey. Problems also arose in the area after a newly laid sewage pipe collapsed, overturning a cart and giving the passengers a ducking. The Rifleman Inn is completely surrounded by water. It was first recorded as the Coach and Horses, but from 1868 to April 1924, when it closed, it was known as the Rifleman. In 1899 it had four private and two public rooms, which were reported as 'very small for the accommodation of customers'. The white building is Southam's Brewery and just to the left of the cottages in the centre was another inn called the Eagle.

Frankwell, January 1899. Although the flood had not reached its peak of 17ft 6in, it shows the difficulties the people in the low-lying parts of Frankwell had to deal with. Coracles were a common sight in Frankwell and were ideally suited for ferrying people and provisions to places where plank walks or ordinary boats could not reach. Neddy Powell, who lived in a cottage near the Barge Gutter, was reputed to have one of the best coracles on the river. During one flood he carried himself, a boy, a hundredweight of coal and a gallon of water to his marooned house in the craft. The photographer is looking down Frankwell Quay. The tall building in the centre was known as the Sweep's House, while the large building on the right is the Welsh Presbyterian chapel. The road between the two buildings led through to the Stew and the Glen. The barber's pole on the left belonged to Johnny Hughes, the first Mayor of Frankwell.

Frankwell, January 1899. A lady stands on the steps of the Sweep's House in Frankwell Quay, watching the river rise slowly up towards her front door. The buildings on the left are still standing today. The house behind the gas lamp is the Plough, which was first recorded in 1883. It was closed in 1906 after the police complained that there were nine other inns within a radius of 190yd and that the house was frequented by people from lodging houses and a very rough class of characters. Just beyond is the Anchor, which was recorded in 1780 and is still open today. The house that juts out at a right angle at the far end is the Model Lodging House, which advertised 'well aired beds' for 1d a night. Until 1890 it was a public house known as the White Horse, which gave its name to a passage leading into Mountfields. The passage in the centre leads through to St George's Buildings. With the large number of public houses in the area the rather fine-looking gentlemen's urinal on the left was aptly named the Frankwell Relief Centre.

Frankwell, January 1899. The people of Shrewsbury were caught totally unprepared by this flood, as it was thought that with the construction of the waterworks and dam on the River Vyrnwy, by the Liverpool Corporation, that another major flood was unlikely. During the evening a man drinking from a bottle and rather unsteady on his feet fell from the planks in Frankwell. After several attempts to reach dry land he was hauled to safety by spectators who were amused that he was more upset about the loss of his bottle of beer than he was about his soaking. The planks also collapsed several times and on one occasion threw a soldier from the barracks into several feet of water. Note the ladder at the window of Harris's tripe shop. To the left is the entrance to Court Nine and then the premises of William Gittens, a cane-chair bottomer, and Johnny Hughes, the barber. The white building on the right, which was occupied by William Pritchard, a local builder, is part of the timber-framed building built at the beginning of the seventeenth century.

The junction of New Street and Frankwell, *c.* 1930. This timber-framed building stood on the corner of New Street and Frankwell until the late 1960s when it was removed to Avonscroft Museum near Bromsgrove. The site is now part of the large Frankwell roundabout. The building was erected by John Worrall in the last quarter of the sixteenth century. In the eighteenth century it became an inn called the Royal Oak, then the Cross Keys, before changing its name to the String of Horses until it was delicensed on 19 July 1907. In 1900 it was owned by Lassells and Sharman's Brewery and managed by John Davies, the last landlord. There was overnight accommodation for four people in two rooms and stabling for five horses. The entrance to the stable yard is through a big arch just beyond the gable on the right. As well as stables the yard also contained five houses in extremely cramped conditions. In 1912 Shrewsbury Co-operative Society opened a shop there. During the alterations a dark oak fireplace with an ornamental brick cornice was uncovered.

Opposite: Howard Street, *c.* 1945. The street takes its name from John Howard, the great eighteenth-century prison reformer, whose bust is displayed over the entrance of Shrewsbury Prison at the top of the hill. The street has also been called Terrace Walk and Castle Hill. This view was taken through the gates of the railway station across to the Butter Market, which was erected at the terminus of the Shrewsbury Canal. The building was designed by Fallows and Hart of Birmingham in the Neoclassical style. The foundation stone was laid by W.H. Griffith on 28 May 1835 and it was completed within the year. The opening by William Jones in May 1836 was followed by a celebration dinner attended by 300 gentlemen and catered for by Mr Lunt the landlord of the Eagle and Tun. The building was converted into a warehouse for the railway in 1857. By the middle of the last century it had fallen into disrepair and was due for demolition. This decision was overturned in 1974 and the building has been transformed into a nightclub and a top venue for world music.

The Toll House, Mytton Oak Road, *c.* 1930. A schoolboy takes his dog for a walk up Crowmeole Lane, towards Mytton Oak Road. The land on which the road runs was once part of the large Mytton estate, but is named after Mytton Oak House that stood close by. The road was named in 1934 and after the opening of the new bypass was soon clogged with traffic. Crowmeole Lane links Mytton Oak Road to Radbrook Road and in a directory for 1936 only three houses are listed on it. They were Sandhurst, Kenlyn and Crowmeole Farm, which was occupied by Thomas Bebb. In 1945 a large council estate was started to the eastern side of the lane and since then most of the lane has been engulfed in housing. The building on the corner is an old toll house. In the 1930s it was known as the Gate House and was occupied by Mrs Killan.

Frankwell, *c.* 1930. These buildings stood on the site of Frankwell traffic island almost opposite St George's Street. The building to the left is part of the String of Horses block which extended down to the corner of New Street. The white sign is advertising the London Central Meat Market. The next pair, nos 31 and 32, were built as one house. A.W. Ward in his book, *Shrewsbury – A Rich Heritage*, describes it as 'one good house; No. 31 rears up its framework in a fine old gable which probably has the steepest pitch of any in town'. In the 1930s it was the home of Edward Owen who was known locally as Neddy Pump, a pump maker, well digger and water diviner. His wife used to supplement their income by catching eels and selling them fresh from a bucket in the town's market. The building was demolished in the 1960s.

Conduit Head, *c.* 1925. This is a view of the Broadwell or Conduit Head, as it is known locally, where drinking water from a number of wells was supplied to Shrewsbury for nearly 400 years. The scheme was started in about 1556 when fresh drinking water was supplied from the wells and transported through 2 miles of wooden pipes to outlets known as conduits that were placed around the town. Over the years the wooden pipes were replaced first by lead and then cast-iron pipes. In 1865 the reservoir near the Quarry Lodge was replaced by new ones on Kingsland. The Corporation also extended the system into Frankwell, Castle Foregate and Castle Fields by adding more pipes and extra conduits. The water was pure and sweet and

even after the new waterworks was opened at Shelton in 1935 people drew water from the old street conduits until the supply was cut off in 1947. The small building, which is erected over the collecting tank, dates from 1578. The following record is attached to the building: 'The olde heade of the conduit leadinge into Shrewsbury was made new agayne with stone and covered with tymber . . . one house of lime or stone of mason's works, covered with good 'branned' tile or slate, 12 feet long and 9 feet broad, 6 feet high from ground to roof.' The conduits were about 4ft tall, very distinctive and made from cast iron. A knob was turned on the left-hand side of the conduit allowing a flow of water to escape from a lion's head on the front. A bowl was fixed at the foot to catch any overflow, which was used to refresh animals as they passed. Written across the front in bold letters was the legend 'waste not want not'.

7

Historic Hostelries

The King's Head, Mardol, *c.* 1945. The inn is situated in one of the most attractive timber-framed houses in town. It has been accurately dated to 1404 but has been altered many times during its history. Once it had two roofs with gable ends and attic windows facing the street. During alterations in 1962 workmen found a priest hole and a number of artefacts. Later refurbishment in 1987 uncovered wall paintings depicting the Last Supper and the Annunciation on an ancient chimney breast. The inn was first recorded in 1780 as the New Inn but changed its name to the King's Head in about 1820, when another inn of that name further up the street closed. The shop to the left was Thomas Smith's café and confectionery shop.

Roushill, *c.* 1899. This view looks towards Smithfield Road. The Horse Shoe Inn stood on the corner of Roushill and a narrow road leading to the abattoir. The inn belonged to Edward Mullard who lived at Weir Hill near Preston Boats. He was a maltster with two malt houses in Roushill and was also the landlord of the inn until March 1894 when he appointed Charles Craston to run it. In 1900 it was a free house brewing its own ale. It had seven private and four public rooms and stabling for thirty horses. It was first recorded as a public house in 1861 but was closed in 1965 just before the area was redeveloped. The area just to the left of the houses is where Richard Davies had his timber yard.

The Slipper Inn, Barker Street, *c.* 1945. The Slipper has had several changes of name during its long history. It was first recorded as the Slipper in 1780, the Hope and Anchor between 1828 and 1835 and the Oddfellows' Arms from 1851 to 1856, reverting to the Old Slipper Inn by 1868. The old inn stood in front of the modern one but was removed for road widening in the 1930s. When the new inn opened it was given this fine sporting sign showing a man known as the Slipper In releasing greyhounds from their leash during a hare-coursing match. During the 1960s the sign was changed to show an eastern-style slipper with a big pom-pom on the toe, completely changing the true name of the inn. Since then it has changed names several times, to Jackson's in 1998, to the Merchant Stores in 2002 and finally to Rowley's in 2005 in honour of the Rowley family whose house and mansion stand opposite.

The Fierce Dragon outside the Crown Hotel, *c.* 1940. The dragon was carved out of solid oak and was the work of a Russian émigré who fled to Britain at the time of the Russian Revolution in 1917. It was painted bright red and had a lantern hung around its neck. The fierce face, out-spread wings and vicious talons used to frighten and intrigue local children who would fight to sit at the front of a double-decker bus that would pass within inches of the monster as it turned out of Pride Hill into St Mary's Street. The dragon decorated the front of the hotel until the building was demolished in 1962. The fate of the dragon is unknown.

The Old Post Office Hotel, Milk Street, *c.* 1940. The hotel is housed in a building up a passageway to the rear of Proude's Mansion, parts of which date back to 1467. The structure of the inn itself is thought to date from the end of the sixteenth century. In 1886 the landlord was John Parry, who was also a maltster and hop merchant, running that part of his business from a building on the corner of Mill Road in Abbey Foregate. The best-known landlord was Sam Powell who took charge in 1937 and remained there until his retirement in August 1965. Over the years he brightened up the entrance to the hotel with baskets and tubs of flowers that won him many awards in the Town of Flowers competition. In 1947 he was elected councillor for the Castle and Stone Ward and in 1959 he became an alderman of the council. He was greatly involved in sport and during his long stay at the Old Post Office the hotel took on a strong sporting theme, with the walls hung with photographs of local athletes, footballers and other sportsmen from the past.

The Lion Tap, Barrack's Passage, *c*. 1900. The inn is housed in a timber-framed building erected in about 1426. The building runs the full length of the passage. Although slightly older than Henry Tudor House that faces Wyle Cop, the two buildings are linked. The inn was first recorded in about 1868 as a beer house attached to the Lion Hotel. Between 1879 and 1883 it was called the Trotting Horse before reverting back to its original name until it closed in 1925. At the beginning of the twentieth century the inn was owned by Trouncer's Brewery which was based in Longden Coleham. The landlord was Robert Weatherby who took charge in 1894 and whose name is on the inn sign. There were five private and three public rooms with accommodation for eight people in four double rooms. The only complaint was that it only had one urinal, and that was not on the premises but situated two doors away. The inn was revived towards the end of the twentieth century and was known again for a short while as the Trotting Horse before changing back to the Lion Tap. The passage has also been known as Elisha's Shut after a family that lived in Henry Tudor House, the building that straddles the entrance at the far end.

Opposite: Wyle Cop, *c*. 1917. London House was first recorded in 1835 and was delicensed in 1925 shortly before it was demolished to make the road wider at the top of the Cop. It was also known as the London Coffee House and the London Commercial and it belonged to a Mr Thomas of Breck Road, Liverpool. It had ten private and four public rooms with overnight accommodation for seventeen people in eight bedrooms. In 1886 the landlady Mrs Wrightson advertised 'Wines and Spirits, Well Aired Beds. Fine Home Brewed Ales. Special Attention Paid To The Comfort Of Travellers'. The building to the left housed the firm of Edwin Cole, painters and decorators, carvers and gilders. Mr Cole was also a very good artist and has left a number of fine paintings depicting the town in the early twentieth century. The passageway leads into Dogpole Court, which contained the office of the Lichfield Brewery Company, the Granville Liberal Club and the home of the two Humphreys sisters.

The rear of the Unicorn, Wyle Cop, *c.* 1910. The Unicorn was housed in a building, parts of which date back to the fifteenth century. In 1804 it was a coaching inn with coaches running to London, Chester, Hereford and Bristol. Note the sign on the right for the Ostler's bell. In the nineteenth century a new bowling green was opened at the rear with great ceremony. It was advertised as an 'Unparalleled Attraction, Positively One Night Only!!' The new green was brightly illuminated with thousands of variegated lamps. A military band performed many popular pieces of music followed by Signor Perziani's 'Gala and Magnificent display of Fireworks'. The highlight of the display was the ascent of the Monster Model Balloon, which rose to a great height before discharging a flight of splendid balloons to the same plan as those despatched in search of Sir John Franklin when he was lost in the Arctic. Admission was 1*s*, children half-price. Through the arch is Attfield's large grain warehouse, now a restaurant known as the Cornhouse.

Opposite: The Barge Hotel, Wyle Cop, *c.* 1940. The Barge Hotel used to stand on the bank of the River Severn to the right of the English Bridge as you leave town. It was recorded from 1780 and has also been called the Bridge Inn. Towards the end of the nineteenth century the landlord, Mr Plowden Pugh, advertised for hire at moderate prices 'Open and closed carriages, Brougham, cabs, gig and dog carts. Waggonette, Whitechapel, pony and Phaeton. Saddle horses for ladies and gentlemen. Excellent stabling, loose boxes, coach houses and good accommodation for tourists, travellers and bicyclists. An ordinary daily'. An ordinary was a dinner served either daily or weekly at an inn, at the same time and for the same price. Mr Pugh's hobby was researching the history of Shrewsbury inns. The inn was rebuilt twice in its history. It closed in 1956 when the licence was transferred to the Springfield on Wenlock Road. The building was demolished in about 1967 to make way for a garage.

The Park Hotel, Abbey Foregate, *c.* 1945. The building has a classical brick skin over an earlier timber frame. It was once the town house of the Hill family of Attingham and can be traced through deeds dating back to 1510. In one of the upper rooms was an ancient tapestry described in *By-Gones* in 1909 as 'in panels of various sizes and is tolerably well preserved although the colours have become faint and dim. Some of the costumes seem to me to be Jacobean and others oriental. The latter appear in scenes which most likely are Biblical. The piece over the fire place represents, I think, King Solomon welcoming the Queen of Sheba.' Unfortunately they were removed and have vanished without trace. The inn closed in about 1960 and the building was converted into a club affiliated to the Labour Party. The name of the inn commemorated the park set up in the monastic grounds during the eighteenth century. To the left is Cyril Crawford's newsagent's and to the rear, Park Cottage, another timber-framed building but with brick infill replacing the wattle and daub.

The Dun Cow, Abbey Foregate, *c*. 1940. Beneath the plaster is a timber-framed building dating from the first half of the seventeenth century. Over the front entrance is a fine figure of a cow, the legendary Dun Cow of Dunsmore Heath that was reported to be 'an exceeding great and monstrous cow, making most dreadful devastation'. It was said to have been slain by Guy, the Earl of Warwick. In 1900 the inn had nine private and four public rooms with stabling at the rear for twenty-four horses. There was overnight accommodation for sixteen people in six bedrooms, and although the inn was reported to be in good condition, there was only one urinal and one WC for the whole house. The inn continues to thrive and is reported to have a friendly ghost who can walk through walls. Betton House to the left has been demolished. In 1896 it was a boys' school run by Thomas Stone, but by 1914 it had been converted into a garage by Legge and Chamier, the sole agents for Wolseley, Stellite, Bedford-Buick and Minerva cars. It was also the first garage in the country to have a roadside petrol pump.

The Heathgates Hotel, Harlescott, *c.* 1940.
The inn was built at the junction of the
busy Whitchurch and Sundorne roads in
the fast-growing suburb of Harlescott. It
was opened in 1938 and its licence was
transferred from the Mermaid in Barker
Street that had been demolished for road
widening. Over the inn sign is a very nice
weathervane depicting a five-bar gate and a
country gentleman with his dog and gun.
The weathervane has since disappeared.
Heathgates is the modern name for Old
Heath that ran north through Harlescott
and Battlefields. From 1591 to 1794 a
gallows was set up in this area for the
execution of felons.

The London Apprentice, Coton Hill, *c.* 1925. The inn was first recorded as the London Apprentice in
1780, a name that it kept until 2001 when it was changed to the Severn Apprentice. The former name
was taken from a famous ballad written in the eighteenth century, which tells of the experiences of a
young apprentice who travelled the world performing such great feats as killing a lion with his bare
hands. Before it was known as the London Apprentice it was called the George Barnwell after another
apprentice from London who is reputed to have robbed his master on three occasions and murdered his
uncle in Ludlow. In 1900 the inn was owned by Worthington & Company, from Burton upon Trent. The
inn had accommodation for eight people in three rooms and held a Smoking Concert every two weeks,
which was by invitation only. The building was demolished in 1959 after the new inn had been built at
the rear.

Frankwell, January 1899. This is a section of Frankwell Quay from Court Eleven on the left, which was also known as Plough Passage to the Mission Room and Court Twelve. The man in the coracle, watched by a number of spectators in the upper bedroom windows, looks as though he is heading for the Plough Inn. Even in these conditions it wasn't unusual for flooded inns to stay open, with customers standing on barrels and tables in a flooded bar or sitting in the bedrooms enjoying their favourite tipple. In 1899 the inn was occupied by Richard Gough and consisted of eight private and three public rooms. There were two entrances, one on the main street and another in the passage where there were also twelve cottages. It is recorded that from such a passage during this flood, two women with newly born babies were rescued with great difficulty and taken to more comfortable surroundings. Part of the house next door has also been an inn called the Dog and Badger. At this period the little shop was occupied by Richard Kynaston, a shoemaker.

Opposite: The Boathouse Hotel, New Street, *c.* 1940. The inn was first recorded in 1806, but its history stretches back further than that. During the seventeenth century it was owned by the Harwood family, who also kept the Old Ship Inn in Bridge Street and owned several barges and trows that worked the Severn from Bristol up to Pool Quay in Wales. When a plague attacked the town in 1650 the building was used as a pesthouse or isolation unit for the parish of St Chad. During the first six months of that year over 250 people from the parish died in the outbreak. Parts of the building are very old, but the frontage was heavily remodelled in the twentieth century.

The Crow Inn, Frankwell, *c.* 1940. The inn stands on the corner of Water Lane and was first recorded in 1780. It was also called the Old Crow, to distinguish it from another Crow Inn at 100 Frankwell that changed its name in 1828 to the New Inn. In 1900 the Crow consisted of seven private and four public rooms, two were used for food only and there was no overnight accommodation, and there was stabling for thirteen horses in the yard at the rear. The inn, which was housed in an early sixteenth-century building, closed in September 1971 and was converted into flats. The building to the right was occupied by Lewis and Froggatt the ironmonger's and cycle dealers. At the rear they had a large indoor arena where customers were taught the art of cycling before they were allowed out on the open road. By the 1930s it had been converted into a garage and taken over by Arthur Charles. In the 1960s it was the home of Rodington Dairy; it is now occupied by an antique dealer.

The Boathouse Inn, New Street, *c.* 1895. From this riverside view of the inn you get the impression you are in the heart of the countryside, but after crossing on the ferry you are just two minutes' walk from the centre of town. A return trip on the ferry cost 1*d*. For many years pleasure boats could be hired from the inn and light refreshment could be obtained from the building on the left. The ferry was decommissioned in 1922 with the opening of the Porthill Bridge, and the pleasure boats disappeared during one of the 1960s floods, never to be replaced. The open land at the rear is part of Oscar Pritchard's nursery, which occupied most of the west side of the street. At the beginning of the twentieth century most of the nursery was sold for building. The site behind the inn is occupied by Sandhurst, once the home of Councillor Samuel Withers.

The Oak Hotel, Shelton, *c.* 1939. The hotel was erected in the art deco style and opened in 1939, not long after the new A5 bypass around Shrewsbury had been built. It was situated at the western end of the bypass and took its name from the Shelton Oak that stood close by. It was from that oak tree that legend tells us the Welsh prince, Owen Glendower, is supposed to have watched the Battle of Shrewsbury raging. In fact at the time he was in South Wales at the siege of Carmarthen. During the 1970s it was a popular rendezvous for the young, having its own disco with ultra-violet lighting. In about 2000 the hotel was demolished and a small estate of luxury houses built on the site.

The Brooklands Hotel, Meole Brace, *c.* 1940. The Brooklands stands to the side of the new Shrewsbury bypass, which was opened on 23 May 1933. The new bypass and the junction of Upper Road are on the right of the hotel. The Brooklands was rebuilt and enlarged on the site of a private house of that name and opened on 6 April 1931. It replaced the Red Lion that was demolished in 1932 as it stood in the path of the new road. One of the Brookland's most memorable landlords was Hubert Morley who spent his life in the licensed trade and was brought up at the Cross Guns in New Street.

The Plough, Belle Vue, *c.* 1940. Before 1868 the Plough Inn was known as the Belle Vue, a name it reverted to for a short while towards the end of the twentieth century before changing back to the Plough. This timber-framed building replaced the old inn during the 1930s. Once, the inn had a nice gilded miniature plough over the doorway. The old horse chestnut tree to the left was blown down in a gale. At one time Belle Vue Road was known as Meole Road.

The Boar's Head, Belle Vue Road, *c.* 1940. Parts of the inn, which has been regularly recorded since 1780, date back to the middle of the seventeenth century. During its history it has been altered and a brick skin now covers the timber frame. Nos 18 and 20 to the left of the Boar's Head have also been listed as licensed premises, either as a beer house or as the Engine and Tender. This inn was closed on 8 August 1910. To the right of the Boar's Head is the entrance to the Boar's Head Yard and the narrow path leading to Egland Cottages. The newsagent's to the right belonged to Edwin Hargest and is in Morton Crescent. The crescent was created in 1932 from the bottom end of Belle Vue Road, and it takes its name from Morton House that stood close by.

8

Military Matters

Chester Street, *c.* 1895. Until 1830 this street was known as Bagley Bridge, although it has also been known as Back Lane. Crowds of people again turn out to see a parade of horsemen in splendid military uniforms ride through the town. The photographer is looking back towards Coton Hill on the left and Cross Street to the right. Five houses were set back on the corner of Cross Street. One of the largest was occupied by Mrs M. Williams who rented out part of her home as apartments. The gateway on the right led into the carriage works of W.G. Mountford who also had other premises in Castle Foregate and was probably connected to the carriage works on Dogpole, reputed to be the oldest in the county, being established in 1819. During the alterations to the railway station between 1899 and 1902 a loading bay for animals was built on the site, which gave easy access to the cattle market on Smithfield Road. The cottages on the right were part of a terrace that was demolished at the end of the 1950s. At this period the end two cottages were occupied by William Wood, a shoemaker, and by Mrs Mary Leek.

Castle Street, *c.* 1895. Great interest is shown by the people of Shrewsbury as the 12th Lancers parade past the Raven Hotel. The hotel stood on that site for about 400 years until it was demolished in 1961. The entrance to the right led to the Raven yard and stables, which were run by Henry Franklin. He also had livery and bait stables on Swan Hill and Cross Hill and was able to supply the public with a variety of superior horses and carriages for all occasions. In 1896 Hall, Wateridge and Owen also had a repository in the yard. Next door is J. Bennett's bookshop and above St James's Temperance Hotel, which was managed by Thomas Barnett. The staff of John Davies's grocery shop are standing in the doorway, watching the parade. Note the smart bow windows of the shop. They would have been commonplace in the town until the 1820s when Shrewsbury Improvement Commission encouraged house and shop owners to install flat ones. The shop with the awnings and the Noah's ark above the second-floor window was run by John Franklin. It was known as the Ark and was a haberdashery, hosiery and wool depot. The right-hand side of the building was an inn called the Talbot Vaults that was there from 1856 to 1896. The name had been revived after the Talbot Hotel closed in Market Street in 1851, in the hope of cashing in on its good reputation.

Vice-Admiral Robert Jenkins CB is talking to two Borough police officers on St Chad's Terrace in 1893. He was attending a service in St Chad's Church to celebrate the wedding of Prince George to Princess Mary of Teck. The family moved to Shropshire from Dorset in 1651 and served in Parliament and in the military and navy. His uncle was Sir Richard Jenkins, MP for Shrewsbury from 1830 to 1833, and again from 1837 to 1841. Robert Jenkins joined the navy as a naval cadet in 1838 and rose quickly through the ranks. He became a Commander of the Baltic in 1864, a Rear Admiral in 1875 and a Vice-Admiral in 1880, the year he retired. During his career he was awarded six medals for distinguished service, two clasps and one decoration, the Companion of the Bath. He became Mayor of Shrewsbury in 1881 but suffered a stroke and was forced to retire after only a few months in office. He lived for many years with his wife in Abbey Foregate, but after the death of his sister he moved back to the family home at Charlton Hill, Wroxeter, where he died on 22 August 1894 at the age of sixty-nine.

The Shropshire Yeomanry in the Square, *c.* 1895. Men of the Shropshire Imperial Yeomanry gather in the Square, probably in 1895, to celebrate their centenary year. At the end of the eighteenth century, with the threat of invasion by the French, regiments of cavalry were formed within a county for home defence and to help the regular army in times of national emergency. The name Yeoman is an ancient word, which denotes a man who farms his own land and is of a higher status than a labourer but lower than a gentleman farmer. It was from this stratum of society that the troops were drawn. The Market Drayton Troop was the first to be formed on 11 January 1795, but owing to a fall in their numbers the honour of being counted first goes to Wellington, which was registered on 17 April and was the sixth regiment to be formed in the country. By 1814 there were eleven units in the county with such colourful names as the Brimstree Loyal Legion, the Oswestry Rangers and the Pimhill Light Horse. By 1814 the smaller units had amalgamated to form three regiments, the Shrewsbury Yeomanry Cavalry, the North Shropshire Cavalry and the South Shropshire Cavalry. In 1828 the regiments merged into two with the South Shropshire and the Shrewsbury Regiments becoming the South Salopian Regiment while the North Shropshire became the North Salopian Regiment. Both regiments combined in 1872 to form the Shropshire Yeomanry Cavalry. Probably its greatest achievements was in South Africa where it formed the 13th Company of the 5th Battalion of the Imperial Yeomanry, winning the Regiment's first battle honours. By the outbreak of the First World War methods of fighting had changed and the days of the cavalry were over, which meant that the Yeomanry had to change and adapt to survive. It was very successful. In April 1998 it celebrated its 200th anniversary at a special service in St Mary's Church where it was given the honour of the Freedom of Shrewsbury. The troops are lined up on three sides of the Square with the public in High Street. Lord Clive's statue, which was unveiled in January 1860, stands in the centre. Note the people watching the scene from the windows of Grocott's shop on the right. Next door is the timber-framed Plough Inn before its top storey was added.

The Racecourse, Monkmoor, c. 1890. The 1st Shropshire and Staffordshire Volunteer Artillery (Position Artillery) was formed at the beginning of the nineteenth century. Its headquarters in 1896 was in Victoria Square, Shelton, Stoke-on-Trent. The Light Brigade Division (1st and 2nd Batteries, Shrewsbury and Wellington) shared its headquarters with the Shropshire Imperial Yeomanry at the Drill Hall and the Riding School in Longden Coleham. The commanding officer of the Shropshire Batteries was Lieutenant-Colonel Edmund Cresswell Peele who came from a prominent local family. He became a solicitor in the family practice and served the town and county in a number of ways including as Town Clerk, County Under-sheriff, Clerk of the County Council and Mayor of Shrewsbury in 1892 and 1897. He is the horseman on the right, leading his men on an exercise. He joined the Artillery Volunteers as a gunner in 1861, was commissioned in 1868 and rose rapidly through the ranks to become Colonel-in-Chief.

The Racecourse, Monkmoor, c. 1890. The Long Mynd Hills served as a firing range for the Shrewsbury and Wellington Batteries, and metal-detecting enthusiasts are still able to find cannonballs and shells embedded in the hillside. The batteries also used the rifle range at Hencote to practise with their carbines and the open fields of Monkmoor to carry out manoeuvres. This view shows a gun crew ready for action at Monkmoor with the wooded tops of Haughmond Hill in the background. The field gun is an Armstrong rifle breech-loader that was introduced in 1885. The corporal in charge stands to the right of the gun. Note his insignia of rank on his left arm and on his pillbox cap.

The Barracks, Copthorne, 1899. The departure of the troops caused quite a stir and a large crowd mainly of youngsters gathered outside the barracks to watch their departure. The main gate is on the right flanked by the guard houses with slit windows. They were demolished a number of years ago when the entrance was remodelled. The large barrack block is at the rear. The barracks was first occupied on 30 December 1881. Over 4 million bricks, all made near the 9-acre site by the contractor, were used in its erection. The cost of the building was in the region of £65,000.

Frankwell, 1899. This is the military band leading the volunteer company through Frankwell to the railway station. The bandmaster was Mr F.G. Rowland who had chosen a varied selection of military music to be played en route. As the men marched through Frankwell, fireworks were lit by Alf Hughes and a cannon was discharged near the Welsh Bridge by Johnny Hughes and Thomas Bryan. Many of the boys who had gathered to see them off at the Barracks marched with them and were aware of the photographer as they approached the Welsh Bridge. The building in the background is now Hall's auction house, which was built on the site of the Squirrel Inn. It was designed in 1887 by A.B. Deakin for Isaac Eakin, a wool and seed merchant. By 1896 the building was being used as a warehouse by Richard Bromley, a corn merchant and Mayor of Shrewsbury in 1925. The door to the left led into Mr Eakin's home, which overlooks the river. It was later turned into a boarding house run by Mrs George and is now the offices for Hall's auction rooms.

Opposite: The Barracks, Copthorne, March 1901. The soldiers assembled outside the barracks are reservists called up to form a volunteer company to fight in South Africa. Of the 409 men called 408 turned up and only 21 of those were medically unfit to serve. After assembling at Copthorne the men were sent to Aldershot before embarking for South Africa onboard the Arawa on 7 November 1899. The men are wearing scarlet tunics with blue collar and cuffs, blue trousers with a narrow red stripe and white leather equipment. Their headgear was either the blue spiked helmet or the black Glengarry cap. The company, under the command of Captain B. Treasure and headed by the band of the First Volunteer Band of the King's Shropshire Light Infantry, marched through the town to the railway station. The first house past the Barracks is Lonsdale House, the home of Richard Bromley, a seed merchant and a former Mayor of Shrewsbury.

Castle Foregate, *c.* 1901. The next two views show the crowds gathered in the streets to welcome home one of the volunteer companies back from the war in South Africa and show areas of the town not usually photographed. The crowds are standing on the station forecourt, which was several feet higher than it is today. The old retaining wall cuts across the centre and there would have been a drop of between 10 and 15ft into Castle Foregate. The two highly ornamented buildings at the rear date from the second half of the nineteenth century. The building to the left was a temperance hotel called the Welcome. In 1908 it was advertised as a commercial and family hotel and restaurant with a refreshment bar serving hot dinners daily. There was also first-class accommodation for cyclists at reasonable charges. Visitors were advised to write in advance to secure a room as the hotel was so popular. The building to the right was built in the Italianate style for Thomas Corbett as a sales department for his agricultural equipment. Note the people standing across the parapet for a better view.

Castle Gates, *c.* 1901. The band has just past Meadow Place and is marching towards the town centre. The sign on the right over the pavement belongs to the Bull's Head, while the white building behind the lamp post is the Castle Vaults. The building with the impressive doorway above is the Congregational church, which was opened on 4 March 1845. This church closed in 1909 when a new building was opened in Coton Hill. It is believed that the pillars to the main door were taken to the new church and used to support the roof of the tower. The old building became the town's first cinema, the Picturedrome, and then the Central Hall. It closed in March 1931 after a fire destroyed a great deal of the interior. The Shrewsbury Drug Stores (left) was a chemist shop run by Henry Pattison. Next door was the Railway Tavern, in business from 1868 to 1907. It then became a newsagent's and tobacconist's, but is now a health food shop known as Wild Thyme.

The Square, 1902. Great crowds gather in the Square and High Street to give a heroes' welcome to the men of the 2nd Volunteer Service Company returning home from the Boer War. The men served in South Africa between 1901 and 1902 and while there chose to wear the slouch hat rather than the familiar cork helmet. The Volunteers had to struggle through the crowds and into the Square amid deafening cheers. There to greet them were the Mayors of Shrewsbury and Hereford, the Earl of Powis, Colonel Kenyon-Slaney and the Revd Mr Drinkwater. After a short service and a welcoming address by the Mayor of Shrewsbury the men paraded back to the barracks before being entertained later that evening to dinner in the Corn Exchange. Patriotic drapes of red, white and blue have been placed across Cartwright's Mansion while people gather in the windows of the new insurance offices next door. The highly ornamented building was designed in a Flemish style by local architect A.E. Lloyd Oswell in 1891, a year after the Alliance Assurance Company and the Shropshire and North Wales Assurance Company amalgamated.

The Square, 9 May 1910. King Edward VII died on Friday 6 May 1910, but the proclamation of King George V did not take place until the following Monday. A dais was erected outside the Shirehall for the civic dignitaries. They included the High Sheriff, Sir Raymond Wilson, the Mayor, Alderman B. Blower, and the Corporation, the Borough Chaplain and the Under-sheriff Colonel Cresswell Peele. Drawn up in front were a guard of honour provided by the King's Shropshire Light Infantry, a cadet corps from Shrewsbury School and the bands of the Shropshire Yeomanry and the Borough of Shrewsbury. The weather was bright but cold and a large crowd assembled. The proclamation was read out by Colonel Cresswell Peele who concluded it with 'God Save the King'. The flag over the Shirehall was raised from half-mast, the buglers sounded the salute, while the military presented arms. The bands played the National Anthem after which the people of Shrewsbury gave three rousing cheers for their new monarch. The man with the white beard on the front row is Mr Ravencroft, the town crier.

The Square, 3 July 1914. Veterans from such campaigns as the Crimea, the Indian Mutiny, China, New Zealand, Afghanistan, Abyssinia, Ashanti, Zululand, Egypt and Burma gathered in the Square to be inspected by King George V who was in town for the Royal Show. Some 35 officers and 150 non-commissioned officers were on parade under the command of Lieutenant Colonel H.W. Lovett, the senior officer. He had taken part in the Zulu, Egyptian and Burma campaigns. The oldest veteran on parade was J. Winder, who had enlisted in 1836 when William IV was on the throne. While in the 4th Foot he saw action in the Crimea. The king spoke to Private J. Doogan of the 1st Dragoon Guards who won the Victoria Cross in 1881 at Laing's Nek in South Africa, where he saved the life of Major-General Brownlow. He also noticed Sergeant Major Kilvert of the 11th Hussars who was badly wounded and nursed by Florence Nightingale. Shropshire was proud of the manner in which it cared for its veterans. Twenty years before, a standing committee had been set up in the county to raise adequate funds to look after all local veterans so that none were in need or had to end their lives in the workhouse.

9

The Royal Show,
Carnivals & Circuses

The English Bridge, 3 July 1914. King George V was escorted around the town to the showground by men from the Shropshire Imperial Yeomanry mounted on their superb horses and wearing their wonderful helmets. The Yeomanry was founded in 1795 with the first troops being raised in Wellington and Market Drayton. Note the signs on the lamp post directing traffic up Abbey Foregate to Wenlock, Ironbridge and London and down Coleham to Church Stretton, Ludlow and Hereford. The signs opposite warn motorists and pedestrians of the dangers of the English Bridge.

Abbey Foregate, 3 July 1914. Thousands of people lined the route from the town centre to the showground in Monkmoor to catch a glimpse of King George V as he passed in his carriage. The people are standing outside Shrewsbury Technical College near the English Bridge. Across the road is the Abbey School and part of the Congregational church. In the centre is the curve of a triumphal arch that was erected over the railway bridge. It was made to look like an ancient gateway built out of stone but was constructed from scaffolding and painted canvas. Outside the abbey the choirs of all the town's churches were gathered, along with hundreds of schoolchildren waving flags. As the king's carriage drew to a halt they sang the national anthem, which could be heard all over the town.

Opposite: Royal Show, Monkmoor, July 1914. The Royal Pavilion, which was transported from show to show, stood close to the site where Monkmoor School was erected. The whole of the interior was fitted by J. & B. Blower, house furnishers, decorators and upholsterers, who had premises on Pride Hill and Castle Gates. They decorated the reception room in the Old English style with heavy wooden beams and decorated plaster moulds. The floor was covered by a large valuable Persian carpet. A Jacobean fireplace stood at one end of the room and the walls were covered with genuine Tudor and Jacobean tapestries loaned by the Royal School of Art Needlework. The large luncheon room was furnished in the Georgian style. The walls were decorated silver-grey with a white dado rail and harmonised exactly with the curtains which were made out of silver-grey velvet. A heavy, handmade Donegal carpet, 35ft long and in shades of old rose and pink, covered the floor. The furniture was made of mahogany in the Chippendale style. The pavilion also had a writing room and a retiring room, which was panelled with a most exclusive wallpaper. The public was allowed to view the pavilion at certain times. The entrance fee was 3d per person, the proceeds being distributed by Blower's among charitable institutions in the town.

Royal Show, Monkmoor, July 1914. This is the showground side of the main entrance pavilion. The photographer is looking towards Abbey Foregate, with Crowmere Road to the left and Monkmoor Road to the right. Rebuilt today the building would straddle the bottom end of Racecourse Avenue, facing Tankerville Street. The pavilion was occupied by the secretary's office, a ladies' room, a post office and the United Counties Bank, which was banker for the Royal Agricultural Society of England and had a local branch on the corner of Castle Street and St Mary's Street in town. This was the third show to be held in Shrewsbury; the first was in 1845 and the second in 1884. Both were held on the Racecourse at Monkmoor: the first made a loss of £2,995, the second a profit of £2,301. A fourth show was held in the town at Sundorne in 1949, attended by Princess Elizabeth and Prince Philip.

Royal Show, Monkmoor, July 1914. Visitors and stockmen mingle in the collecting ring as cattle are prepared for their big moment in the main arena. Two bandsmen also take advantage of a break to view the attractions of the site. Throughout the five days of the show, music was provided by the band of the 1st Battalion King's Shropshire Light Infantry under the bandmaster, Mr A.J. Wilson. They had three sessions a day playing from the central bandstand near the main arena so that an assortment of military and popular music drifted over the entire showground.

Royal Show, July 1914. Crowds gather in the main arena to watch the parade of cattle. At this show there were 136 classes of cattle, which included Aberdeen Angus, Red Poll, Sussex and Dexter as well as the more common breeds of Hereford and Jersey. Prize money for each class was £10 for first place, £6 for second and £4 for third. One expert noted 'at Shrewsbury in 1914 the dairy cattle breeds were beginning to indicate that trends were changing, and that the Friesian, the Dairy Shorthorn and the Channel Islands breeds were attracting national attention to the detriment of the breeds which had long been associated with certain well-defined areas'. A local winner was W.B. Trudge of Onibury who secured the premier prize for his Hereford bull, Renown, who was calved in 1912. Another locally reared animal was Silver Mist III who won the championship prize for a Shorthorn bull. He was owned by Sir Herbert Leon of Bletchley Park but reared by T.H. Swire of Market Drayton.

Royal Show, July 1914. This was the 75th show to be held and it took place over five days between Tuesday 30 June and Saturday 4 July. The President of the show was the Earl of Powis, the Lord-Lieutenant of Shropshire, who was there to greet the king when he arrived on the Friday. Ticket prices varied. On Tuesday admission was 5s, on Wednesday and Thursday 2s 6d and on Friday and Saturday 1s; or you could buy a season ticket for 10s 6d. With prize money of £11,700 the show attracted 3,394 animals, the second-highest entry of livestock ever. There were also 5,428 agricultural implements on exhibition, at rest and in motion. Unfortunately, even with all these attractions and a visit by the king, the show could only draw a total attendance of 87,803, the worst since 1905, which resulted in a loss of £3,616.

The Royal Show, Monkmoor, July 1914. This is a view of the top end of the showground near to where Abbot's Road is now situated. On the left is the Model Farm, which was built from foundation to roof entirely out of concrete. The living accommodation consisted of a parlour, living room, scullery, larder and dairy on the ground floor, with three bedrooms and a box room on the first. After the show the farm was managed by a tenant for the County Council until it was demolished in about 1953. The show brought visitors from all over the world. Twenty-four Siberian farmers were delighted to have the opportunity of viewing such a large collection of agricultural implements. They were also interested in the cattle and dairy farming, which was carried out in their country on a cooperative scheme, with their farms exporting over 40,000 tons of butter to Britain every year.

Shrewsbury Library, Castle Street, *c.* 1895. Shrewsbury School was founded by Edward VI in 1552. Under the charter the school was to be endowed with the tithes which had been paid to the Colleges of St Mary and St Chad, amounting to £20 8*s*. The bailiffs and burgesses were to appoint the two masters, and with the advice of the Bishop of Coventry and Lichfield draw up the rules of government and finance. The site for the school was bought from John Proude for £20. The school moved from this site in 1882 and the buildings were converted into the Shrewsbury Free Library and Museum, which was opened in 1885. The maypole dancers could be from a local school or perhaps one of the attractions of the annual Cycle Carnival.

The Cycle Carnival, *c*. 1900. The amount of time and effort that has gone into the creation of this lady's cycle and dress is incredible and must have taken many weeks of hard work. Every inch of the bike was decorated except for the tyres. The competitors were put into different classes and judging took place on the cattle market before the carnival paraded around the town. There were two parades, one at 3.30 p.m. and another at 7 p.m. The afternoon parade travelled around the town before crossing the English Bridge into Abbey Foregate, returning to the Smithfield via Town Walls. The evening illuminated procession left from Abbey Foregate and crossed the Welsh Bridge into Frankwell, New Street and the very narrow Chapel Street before heading back to the Market Hall for the evening promenade concert and prize giving. Note the livestock in the cattle pens and the house to the right on Smithfield Road.

Cycle Carnival, Smithfield Road, *c.* 1900. The Babes in the Wood look rather dejected sitting in the stocks waiting for the parade to begin. The smartly dressed young boy appears to be from another float, as the sign on his pole reads, Group of Popular Songs and Plays. In 1900 there were twenty-three different categories for competitors from an individual with a decorated bike to the best tableau on a vehicle or on foot with no fewer than ten schoolchildren. Prize money varied between £5 and 2*s* 6*d* but the best prize was a silver challenge shield worth £25 plus £3 in cash for the best decorated vehicle. There were also nine classes with prizes of 10*s* 6*d* for the people who collected money during the parade. One of the classes was for nurses from the hospitals and another for those collecting with poles, who would extract money from people watching from first-floor windows. The float is on Smithfield Road, outside Marshall Brothers, which was listed as a monumental sculptor and mason.

The Cycle Carnival, *c.* 1905. The Shrewsbury Arcadian Morris Dancers were very popular, and in various parts of the town the parade would pause while they performed for spectators. The captain of the team was A.F. Picken and the dancers were Messrs George, Edmunds, Jones, Wiseheart, Trott, Probert, Elleker, Ponchaud, Miller, H. Bayley, S. Bayley and Ward. The group also had their own band with Mr Stockdale on the drum, Mr Friend on the cornet and Mr Laidler on the clarinet. In 1904 the dancers won first prize for the best troupe. As part of the carnival celebrations a fancy dress ball was held at the Music Hall, there were promenade concerts in the afternoons and evenings and a concert

was put on in the Market Hall, where for the price of 6*d* you were entertained by the Shrewsbury Brass Band, a variety balancing act by Mr Wallace Chune, a party of glee singers, the Arcadian Morris Men and the Neapolitan Organ Grinders (below), who were raining money for the Salop Infirmary.

The River Carnival, 17 September 1931. Sabrina, the goddess of the River Severn, cruised sedately downstream with her handmaidens from Coton Hill to the Gay Meadow. She was met there by the Mayor, Alderman William Gowen Cross, and other members of the town council and with a fanfare of trumpets she officially opened the carnival. She proceeded downstream in a decorated barge rowed by eight oarsmen and escorted by six ancient Britons in coracles. After the opening she headed the carnival procession through the streets of the town in her war chariot escorted by the Shropshire Yeomanry. Joan Conday of Victoria Street was chosen to play the part of Sabrina at a carnival ball at the Music Hall. Her handmaidens were Lilly Templeton of Ellesmere Road and Gwen Speake of York Street, Oswestry. Sabrina was dressed in 'a virginal robe of ivory silk trimmed in gold braid in Greek key pattern and a gorgeous cloak of purple'. The attendants wore mauve dresses and orange cloaks. The bargemen were members of the Pengwern Boat Club and the coracle men were from the Sabrina Angling Club. The man with the tricorne hat is Jack Ramsey, Shrewsbury's official town crier in the 1930s.

The English Bridge, *c.* 1898.
People line the pavement to watch as
two excited boys follow the elephant
over the English Bridge and back to
the circus ground on the Gay
Meadow. The elephant probably
belonged to Lord John Sanger's
Colossal Circus and Hippodrome. The
circus, which was regarded as one of
the finest circuses on earth, was
formed by Lord John into a limited
company in 1898 with capital of
£125,000. Two performances were
given each day, in the afternoon and
evening, when a captivated audience
was treated to a brilliant company of
artists and animals performing in the
big top. In addition the people of
Shrewsbury were also invited to view
the free menagerie or watch the grand
procession through the streets of
Shrewsbury every day at 1 p.m.
The people are standing in front of
William Williams's confectionery
shop, the last building before the
bridge. Note the adverts for Fry's
chocolate and ice cream.

The English Bridge, *c.* 1898. Lord George Sanger's circus was a regular and welcome visitor to Shrewsbury during the late nineteenth century. The two sites available to pitch his giant big top were either on the Gay Meadow or in St Julian's Friars. The Gay Meadow was the most popular as it was near the ford on which the English Bridge is built and a good place to water and bathe the animals. Two young lads stand at the water's edge to watch the elephants, camels and horses being watered. Large crowds would also line the bridge to watch the animals and trainers, who would encourage the elephants to spray the onlookers with a trunk full of water. In March 1898 the circus ran foul of the law when it tried to enter the town on a Sunday morning, breaking a law banning wagons in the streets of the Borough on the Sabbath. A lone Borough policeman stopped the convoy on the London Road, and although it had less than a mile to travel, refused to let it pass and sent it packing back to Wellington.

10

Bits & Pieces

The Bear Steps, Fish Street, *c.* 1910. A lady poses at the foot of the Bear Steps in
Fish Street. The ancient thoroughfare that leads from Fish Street through to
St Alkmund's churchyard was named after an inn that stood opposite on the corner of
Grope Lane between 1780 and 1910. The buildings stand right at the heart of
medieval Shrewsbury. Part of the complex, on the bend of Fish Street and Butcher
Row, has been identified as the oldest timber-framed building in the town, dating from
about 1358. In the 1960s the buildings had fallen into such a state of disrepair that
they were in danger of falling down. While under the threat of demolition the newly
formed Civic Society stepped in and raised the funds to save them in 1968.

Leopard Shut, *c.* 1900. This was the first of four passageways between Pride Hill and Roushill. It ran between 3 and 4 Pride Hill and took its name from the Leopard Inn that occupied a building at the mouth of the passage between 1780 and 1883. The shut was later renamed Purslow's Passage after a tailor who opened a shop at No. 3. The remains of Bennett's Hall are in the background, which date from the thirteenth century. The hall was also known as the Old Mint, but there is no evidence that the building was ever used for making coins. The steps are thought to lead into the chapel as there is a small stoop, a bowl for holy water, cut into the right-hand side of the doorway. The remains of the doorway, a large sandstone grate and part of the undercroft still survive in the modern shop built on the site in the 1960s.

Golden Cross Passage, *c.* 1920. This passage is one of the town's ancient shuts and a shortcut between Princess Street and High Street. It takes its name from the inn, which is reputed to be one of the oldest in Shrewsbury, with records of alcohol being served there in 1495, as the bailiff's accounts record '13s-2d in wine, spent on the King's gentlemen in Sextre'. Originally the inn and the passage were known as the Sextry, derived from Sacristy, a place where the church valuables and records were kept, and until 1794 a covered way above Princess Street, connected the inn to old St Chad's Church. Another name for the passage in the eighteenth century was Stillyard or Steelyard Shut. This name crops up in other towns and indicates a place where foreign merchants would gather to trade. It took its present name in about 1795. Parts of the timber-framed inn date from about 1500 but the stone doorway on the left is thought to be part of an older building. This view looks towards High Street before the buildings over the passage were altered.

Compasses Passage, Wyle Cop, *c.* 1920. This is one of four of the town's shuts that linked Wyle Cop to Back Lane, the modern Belmont Bank. The first, at the top of Wyle Cop, is Barrack's Passage, which is the largest and the only one that is still a thoroughfare. Near the bend in the hill between Nos 70 and 71 is Compasses Passage, which took its name from the inn that stood to the right of the entrance between 1883 and 1906. The shut remained open until about the middle of the twentieth century. Two further shuts were situated lower down the bank, but both are now closed off on Belmont Bank. The first was Bowdler's Passage and the second School Passage, both referring to Bowdler's School, situated on the corner of Beeches Lane and Belmont Bank.

The interior of the Council House, *c.* 1920. The oldest part of the Council House dates back to the middle of the fifteenth century, when it was erected in part of Shrewsbury Castle's outer bailey. It was remodelled in 1502 by Peter Newton, who was President of the Council of the Marches. It was known as Lord's Place and was used by the President of the Council as a dwelling and for meetings when the council was away from its headquarters in Ludlow Castle. It was the home of Philip Sidney, the famous Elizabethan poet and soldier, whose father was President of the Council. In 1689 the council was dissolved and the house fell into disrepair until it was converted into three dwellings. In the nineteenth century it was the home of Dr William Clement, an eminent surgeon and MP, whose memorial stands at the Greyfriars end of the Quarry. His hobby was collecting old oak carvings and panels, which he used to embellish his home. In 1934 it became the home for the Catholic Bishop of Shrewsbury but is now a private house.

The interior of Drapers' Hall, St Mary's Place, *c.* 1920. The Drapers were a group of extremely wealthy and powerful businessmen who held the monopoly for trading in Welsh cloth and for exporting it abroad through the London market. The Shrewsbury Drapers are first mentioned in the early years of the thirteenth century and were granted a royal charter by Edward IV in 1462. The original hall was a modest affair, erected in 1485 at a cost of £9 15s 6d. As their wealth and power increased they built a new hall on the same site to reflect this, and for over four centuries it has been the centre for all their business, charitable and social activities. The main hall still contains a great deal of its original furnishings, including a 17ft-long oak table, made in 1632 by Francis Bowyer for £2 15s. Two years later he made matching benches for £3. The painting on the left depicts Edward IV and was painted by Thomas Francis in 1660.

The rear of the Abbot's House, Butcher Row, *c.* 1920. This area has altered beyond recognition. In the nineteenth century there were several cottages at the rear and conditions were very insanitary. Julia Wightman, the wife of the vicar of St Alkmund's, visited a sick parishioner here and found chickens roosting on the bedstead. On 21 June 1851 she records in her diary that she went to visit an old man on his deathbed and 'shall never forget the scene. I went up the stairs unmolested; the bedroom door was open, but in vain did I knock, or ask for admittance. The noise within was quite terrible – it was that of drunken mirth, the room was in disorder; the sick man as he sat up in bed, held a glass of brandy and water in his uplifted hand, flourishing it in high style – he was shouting – his wife was very merry.'

Court House, Mountfields, *c.* 1920. Court House is a substantial Georgian building that once belonged to the Drinkwater family. Richard Drinkwater gave the land for the building of St George's Church in 1832 and his son Charles was vicar there for over fifty years, from 1872 to 1923. The house, which occupies the site of a much older building, was later home to George Henry Eldred, the owner of Eldred Mottram & Company, the tent and marquee specialists founded in 1790. The stone pillars at the front door once adorned an old building at the top of Mardol, which was demolished in 1867 when the site was cleared for the new Market Hall.

The Eye, Ear and Throat Hospital, Murivance, *c.* 1910. Shrewsbury's first Eye and Ear Hospital was opened in a private house in Castle Street in 1818. It moved to a building just below the Welsh tabernacle on Dogpole in 1867 and to this more permanent building in 1881. It was designed by C.O. Ellis of Liverpool in the popular Gothic design and built out of Ruabon brick with a terracotta dressing. It cost in the region of £12,000, which was raised by public subscription. The Countess of Bradford performed the opening ceremony using a silver key which was later exhibited by the main door. The hospital was extended to the right in the same style in about 1925 and was opened by Princess Mary, the Princess Royal. The hospital closed in June 1998 when a new head and neck unit was opened at the Royal Shrewsbury Hospital. The building has been converted into town houses, and during the alterations many of the original features such as the spire were restored. To the left is the concourse to the Kingsland Bridge, which was opened in 1882.

Work on the sewage system, *c.* 1900. Some disruption was caused in the main streets of the town as a network of sewage pipes was laid. One of the main obstacles was how to get the waste across the river to the pumping station and out to the new sewage farm at Monkmoor. In this view workmen are laying the new pipeline across the river just above the English Bridge, with Marine Terrace on the left. At first the plan was to have the pumping station and the sewage farm on one site, but it was found that a great deal of money could be saved if the pumping station was put nearer to the source of sewage. The new system was planned by John Taylor, Sons and Santo Crimp a firm of civil engineers from London. The pumping station was equipped with two steam-powered beam engines that were constructed by W.R. Renshaw of Stoke-on-Trent. They pumped the waste to the top of Whitehall Street where gravity took over, taking it down to the sewage farm. The scheme, which was opened by the Mayoress, Mrs Mary Scotlock-Hughes, on 1 January 1901, cost about £70,000.

Longden Coleham, c. 1900. Work is well under way in the building of the pumping station on the banks of the Severn in Longden Coleham. It was part of a scheme to rid the town of sewage instead of depositing it into the river. During hot dry summers before the weir was built the waste was not flushed downstream, which led to wide-scale pollution and an appalling stench around the town. The site was bought from John Davies for £685 and was occupied by cottages facing the main road with gardens running down to the river. The large building on the left is the rear of the woollen mill built in about 1790. It was later converted into a cotton mill by Charles Hulbert but the venture proved unsuccessful and the property was turned into houses and workshops. In 1889 part of the building was converted into the Brush Factory by John Hudson Davies. The factory was founded in Mardol in 1818 and provided a variety of brushes and brooms, including its speciality, the Madagascar Bass Broom. The building was demolished in 1939. The building to the right is the Cross Foxes, which was first recorded in 1883. In 1906 the Borough police wanted to close it down. One of the reasons for this was that the landlord had been indiscreet during elections by giving customers who voted in a certain way The Long Pull, which meant that their glasses were filled with more beer than those who voted in another way. Another reason the police wanted to close it down was that there were too many hostelries in the area. The house to the left was the Plough and Harrow, which was recorded from 1780 to 1936. The inn was demolished and a new building built further back from the road.

St Mary's Place, *c.* 1890. Until the middle of the twentieth century the town and the countryside were linked much closer than they are today. Cattle and sheep being herded through the streets of Shrewsbury was a common sight until 1959 when the cattle market moved from Smithfield Road out to Harlescott and a farmer leading a bull by the nose through the town would have hardly turned a head unless it was to admire the magnificent beast. Behind the farmer is Windsor House, which dates mainly from the eighteenth century. It has a fine door frame with carved Ionic pillars, attractive plaster ceilings and an unusual curved wall at the corner. The building in the background stands near the site of the Nurses' Home that was erected in 1912 and has now been turned into apartments. The site was once occupied by the Stone House. The original house was built of stone in the sixteenth century on the old town wall, but during the eighteenth century it was greatly altered with most of the frontage being faced in brick.

Princess Street, *c.* 1890. The Alliance Assurance Company fire engine and crew pose outside the Young Women's Christian Association Hostel in Princess Street. The engine and the horse were kept at the fire station attached to Franklin's Livery Stable on Cross Hill. The men were part-time firemen, all having other jobs. The man standing in the middle is Edward Vaughn the superintendent of the brigade until his retirement at the age of seventy-five in 1918. To supplement his income he was a whitesmith, mending a variety of household items, gas fittings, water pipes and tin goods from his workshop in Music Hall Passage. A second fire crew was employed by the Royal Insurance Office and had their fire station on the corner of High Street and Mardol Head. In 1917 the Borough police force took responsibility for firefighting duties within the town, acquiring all the equipment from the two brigades and a large sum of money from the insurance companies to set up a new fire station under the Market Hall in Claremont Street.

Wesley House, Fish Street, *c.* 1920. Hidden beneath the plaster of the upper storey is a timber-framed building dating from about 1500. The building is jettied, but this has been obscured by brickwork on the ground floor. John Wesley, the founder of Methodism, preached in this house when he visited the town for the first time on 1 March 1761. He travelled from Wednesbury and records in his diary that he was met by a large crowd, 'but they only came to stare. Yet part of them came in; almost all that did (a large number) behaved quietly and seriously.' The next day at 5 a.m. he preached to a large congregation before setting off to Wolverhampton on a borrowed horse. Between 1761 and 1790, the year before he died, he visited Shrewsbury on seventeen occasions. The opening to the left is Bank Passage that leads down to High Street. It takes its name from the Birmingham and District Counties Bank that was situated at the High Street end until about 1910. Before that it was known as Twenty Steps Shut, although today there are just fifteen steps in the passage.

Marine Terrace, *c.* 1930. Marine Terrace was built on a quay next to the English Bridge, which was known at different times as Bulgerlode, the Gulph or the Stone Wharf. The terrace was built by John Stant in the early part of the nineteenth century. He once lived in one of the houses and for a short while the row was known as Stant's Terrace. The fine summer-house was older and was part of Marine Court. It dates from the early eighteenth century and was built in the garden of Jones's Mansion, an older timber-framed house that stood across the road on the other corner of the English Bridge. It was described briefly by Nikolaus Pevsner as 'a square two-storeyed brick gazebo with quoins overlooking the river'. It was demolished in the 1950s, but a similar building survives on Town Walls. They were used as places to relax and entertain friends in a less formal environment. In 1896 the court was occupied by George Williams, a gardener, L. Hildidge, a blacksmith, and Emmanuel Inskip, a sawyer, who probably worked at the timber yard next door.

Darwin House, The Mount, *c.* 1900. This large Georgian house was built by Dr Robert Darwin in 1800. It was originally known as Mount House. It was there on 12 February 1809 that Charles Darwin, the eminent scientist and author of *The Origin of Species*, was born. The ground for the house had been marked as the proposed site for the new Shrewsbury Prison and for many years had been used locally as a rubbish dump. Over the years the doctor established a beautiful and exotic garden overlooking the River Severn and it was there that the young Charles developed his love of botany and science. The last Darwin to live at the Mount was Charles's sister, Susan, who died in 1866. In about 1900 the name of the house was changed to Monkmoor House by Colonel Phillips, who had once occupied a house on Monkmoor Road, but by 1928 it had been renamed Darwin House. The owner at this time was J.K. Morris & Company which bought the property as a recreational centre for their staff and later built a cul-de-sac of houses, called Darwin Gardens, in the lower part of the garden.

Shrewsbury Castle, *c.* 1920. The castle was built overlooking the town's most vulnerable point, the only natural land route into the town. There was a castle here in Saxon times, but this was enlarged by the Normans and expanded over the years into the sandstone structure we see today. After the Welsh had been subdued the castle was neglected, being described as 'very much out of repair' in 1366 and as 'ruinous' in 1399. During the Civil War some renovations were carried out and it was garrisoned by Royalists until the town fell to the Parliamentarians in 1645. In 1787 Thomas Telford restored the castle and converted it into a dwelling for Sir William Poultney, Shrewsbury's MP. It was lived in until 1924 when it was purchased by the Shropshire Horticultural Society and presented to the Borough who converted it into a council chamber, destroying a great deal of Telford's internal work in the process. In 1985 the building was transformed into a Regimental Museum under the expert eye of Geoff Parfitt. It was bombed by the IRA in 1992 but has been restored to its former glory, mapping out the histories of all the Shropshire regiments.

Above and opposite: Archdeacon Owen's Chapel, Swan Hill, *c.* 1925. Swan Hill House was once the home of Archdeacon Hugh Owen, vicar of St Julian's Church. He was co-author, with his fellow cleric John Brickdale Blakeway, the vicar of St Mary's Church, of the *History of Shrewsbury*, published in 1825. At the rear of his house in his large garden he erected a summer house. It was built out of ancient stone and brick and decorated inside and out with carved wood and stone, oak panels, stained glass and other artefacts he had acquired after the fall of St Chad's, from the demolition of St Julian's and St Alkmund's and from other ancient sites around the district. By the 1930s the house was the home of Mrs Wynne-Corrie and few people knew of the summer house's existence until it was discovered in a dilapidated state and in danger of collapse by Dr Barker of Salisbury Cathedral. His search for old stained glass for the cathedral led him to Swan Hill where he found a good quantity, but mostly in fragments apart from a large coat of arms of the Merchant Adventurers. Back at his workshop in Salisbury he succeeded in piecing together some very fine portraits. Although he had spoken to the appropriate ecclesiastical authorities and alerted the local authorities, there was considerable feeling in the town against the removal of the glass and especially two fourteenth-century oak screens that had also been taken. The cathedral kept the glass but rejected the screens, as the Dean of Salisbury doubted if screens displaying medieval art from Shropshire could be made to harmonise with the surroundings of Salisbury. Part of the shrine to St Winifred that had been found in the summer house was returned to the abbey. It had been recycled into the gateway of the English Bridge after the dissolution of the abbey, but found its way to Swan Hill when the bridge was rebuilt in the 1770s. In 1938 Dr Barker wrote to the *Chronicle* to inform it that a great deal of the glass had originated from Winchester College Chapel and that one section representing King Ahaz from the Jessie window had been renovated and returned to the chapel after an absence of 122 years.

Gibbons' Mansion, at the rear of Wyle Cop and Dogpole, *c.* 1940. Gibbons' Mansion was built in 1570 for Sir Nicholas Gibbons, a lawyer who was Bailiff of Shrewsbury in 1588 and 1596. During the Civil War the family were loyal to the Crown and when Charles I visited the town to raise money and troops for his cause, Richard Gibbons helped to secure a loan of £600 for the king. After the town fell to Cromwell's forces Gibbons was arrested, deprived of his aldermanship and expelled from the town. During the nineteenth century the house was occupied by Betton and Evans, the stained-glass experts, whose work can be seen in St Mary's Church, Lichfield Cathedral and Winchester College Chapel. The mansion was damaged by fire on 15 April 1943 when it was being used as a paint store by Charles Credland. When the NFU (National Fire Service) arrived flames were shooting through the roof and it took firemen over an hour to bring it under control. The building was taken down and stored by the council, which had intended to re-erect it at the top of Butcher Row where the public toilets are now situated.

BIBLIOGRAPHY

Barker, J., *Shrewsbury Free Churches*, Brown & Brinnand, *c.* 1900

Forrest, H.E., *The Old Houses of Shrewsbury*, Wilding & Son, 1920

——, *The Old Churches of Shrewsbury*, Wilding & Son, 1920

Hobbs, J.L., *Shrewsbury Street Names*, Wilding & Son, 1954

Kelly's Directories of Shropshire (various dates)

Mercer, E., *The Shropshire Experience*, Logaston Press, 2003

Moran, M., *Vernacular Buildings of Shropshire*, Logaston Press, 2003

Morriss, R.K. and Hoverd K., *The Buildings of Shrewsbury*, Sutton, 1993

Riley, G., *The World's Wonder Show*, Shropshire Horticultural Society, 1988

Shrewsbury Chronicle (various dates)

Shropshire Archaeological Transactions (various dates)

Shropshire Star (various dates)

Simcox, K., *A Town at War*, Shropshire Libraries, 1983

Trinder, B. (ed.), *Victorian Shrewsbury*, Shropshire Libraries, 1984

Ward, A.W., *Shrewsbury, A Rich Heritage*, Wilding & Son, 1946

——, *The Bridges of Shrewsbury*, Wilding & Son, 1935

Wilding's Directories of Shrewsbury (various dates)

ACKNOWLEDGEMENTS

I am very grateful to Mary White, Museums Manager, and Peter Boyd, Collections Manager, of the Shrewsbury Museums Service based in Rowley's House, for giving me access to their vast collection of photographs and lantern slides. I would also like to thank Phil Scoggins, Museum Education Project Officer, for assisting me to sort through the collection and for information concerning some of the photographs. My thanks also goes to Lieutenant-Colonel Roger Allan Garrad for two photographs from a collection he recently donated to the museum and to Bill Lloyd, the landlord of the Cross Foxes in Longden Coleham, for two unique photographs connected with the building of the Coleham pumping station at the beginning of the twentieth century. Last but not least my thanks go to that wonderful team of archivists at the Shropshire Records and Research Centre for all their help in accessing material for writing this book.